YOUR CAREER REVOLUTION

A gift from
Gary Huppert
Career Ownership Coach
@ The Entrepreneur's Source

Learn how to take control of your career, scan
this QR to visit my website and learn more.

YOUR CAREER REVOLUTION

Reimagine and Reclaim the Life of Your Dreams

TERRY POWELL

and The Entrepreneur's Source Career
Ownership Coaches

Published by Ethos Collective™
PO Box 43, Powell, OH 43065
Ethoscollective.vip

Identifiers:

LCCN: 2022916231
Paperback ISBN: 978-1-63680-092-9
Hardback ISBN: 978-1-63680-093-6
eBook ISBN: 978-1-63680-094-3

Available in paperback, hardback, and e-book

DEDICATION

We dedicate this book to the tens of thousands of clients who have allowed us to guide them through their Journey of Discovery—courageous people who have made their dreams come true by taking the path less traveled. You inspire us every day. May you, the reader, also achieve your dreams, and may this book empower you and assist you in your journey.

—The Entrepreneur's Source Career Ownership Coaches

To Bud Hadfield who challenged me to sharpen my arrowhead and get to work, which has made all the difference in my entrepreneurial journey.

—Terry Powell

CONTENTS

Note to the Reader: The New Way for the New World ix
Introduction: Great For Kids Taboo For Adults xiii

PART 1: REVOLT 1
Chapter 1: Welcome to the Career Revolution 3
Chapter 2: Write Your Own Success Story 20

PART 2: REIMAGINE 41
Chapter 3: Discover What Holds You Back 43
Chapter 4: Make the Best Choice for You 58
Chapter 5: No One Needs to Walk Alone 73

PART 3: RECLAIM 87
Chapter 6: There's No Time Like the Present 89
Chapter 7: Case Studies that Clarify 99

Next Steps: Growth Is a Never-Ending Journey 113
Appendices 117
Notes 123
Back Ads 127
About the Author 133
About the Entrepreneur's Source 135

NOTE TO THE READER

THE NEW WAY FOR THE NEW WORLD

Nearly a decade ago, in our pre-pandemic world, we witnessed a trend spreading across the vocational landscape.

To help people navigate this trend, our team wrote a book called *Your Career 2.0*. We wanted to give readers hope and more fulfilling options in a world where Corporate America had broken the social contract with its employees. Remember those days?

The book was released while many people were still picking up the pieces of their lives, trying to make sense of what had happened to their investments, their assets, and their jobs. This Great Recession, created by the subprime mortgage crisis, gave people permission to pause and reconsider their current place in life.

During this time, we saw so many people caught in The Battered Career Syndrome® and The Battered Investor Syndrome®. These aren't the normal dinner table conversation topics. And even though people might not have recognized the diagnosis, plenty of them were familiar with the symptoms. People who suffered from these two syndromes kept going back to hopeless situations with the expectation that this time around they would be different—that the job and the stock markets would go back to the heydays enjoyed in years past.

The book resonated with thousands of people and catapulted a movement. The movement itself began in 1984 when I founded The Entrepreneur's Source with the belief that there had to be a better way for everyday people to become financially self-sufficient. At the time, however, I wasn't sure exactly what that would look like yet. But I thought, *what if we educated people and made them aware of what's possible so they could discover their options?*

People told me not to waste my time with those tire-kickers and dreamers. For me, the word "dreamers" really stuck. I could identify with that; I saw myself as a dreamer too. I discovered that about 75 percent of the adult population has a strong to very strong desire to be self-sufficient. They are all seeking a better way. But only about 5 percent are ready, willing, and able to do something about that desire. The other 70 percent would, too, but they are unsure of where to go, what to do, and whom to trust. Those people could benefit from coaching. Through our trials and tribulations, I am proud to say not only were we the first coaching firm of its kind in the early eighties (we were, in fact, among a very few who even knew what coaching was back then), but we have evolved to become North America's leading Career Ownership Coaching Community. In the past forty years, not only have we had the great privilege of coaching tens of thousands of seekers, but we've also seen highs and lows of economic fluctuations, political upheaval, and the impact of events worldwide. When the Great Recession took so many unsuspecting people by surprise, they needed resources like *Your Career 2.0* to recover from the shock and create a new path for their future.

Since that book released, however, much has changed.

We've encountered wars, pandemics, recessions, the Great Resignation, and many other global events that have once again altered the way people work and live.

Some of those changes were (and are) simply more of the same. The ups and downs of the job market, for example, continue to cause upheaval:

- increased layoffs
- jobs lost to cheaper labor in other countries and entire industries moving overseas
- entire industries disappearing

As job security evaporated—again—so did pension plans. Our families, our incomes, our emotional well-being, and the way we must plan for the future were all drastically affected—again. Maybe you witnessed cutbacks in your company. Or maybe you were lucky enough to survive them, but you wonder when your turn is coming. Perhaps you're currently unemployed or underemployed. Increased levels of fear and uncertainty in today's workplace don't leave much room for inspiration or empowerment.

Over the past few years, it became increasingly apparent that we needed to write a different book for a different time. We've kept the best parts of our original book, *Your Career 2.0*, and we've updated and expanded other parts to navigate this new era.

Despite these sober headlines, not everyone is hopeless and confused—quite the opposite. A growing segment of the population is hopeful and clear about the future. We're excited about what the future holds because, as you'll soon realize, you're the one who has the power to create your new future.

Welcome. We've been waiting for you. We're honored to walk with you on this journey. Like you, we believe in a different way and a different world. Let's jump into *Your Career Revolution*. Shall we?

INTRODUCTION

GREAT FOR KIDS
TABOO FOR ADULTS

"What do you want to be when you grow up?" Remember being asked that question as a child? This one question dominates the hearts and minds of people everywhere. When we're young, we're encouraged to dream about the grand possibilities the future might hold. When we get a little older, however, the same question can feel unsettling. It's one we begin to wish people wouldn't ask us.

Who created the rule that people must have life all figured out by a certain age? I don't know about you, but I haven't stopped growing, nor do I want to. I'm committed to keep progressing and developing until the day I die. Why can't we keep dreaming about what we want to be and what we want to do when we grow up? Why shouldn't we keep evolving as we grow?

The answer, to me, is clear. We must continue to grow.

After all, what's the alternative? Just look around, and you'll see. Bestselling author, John C. Maxwell, puts it this way, "Most people are dead; they just haven't made it official." Benjamin Franklin, George Patton, G. E. Marchand, and many others are often credited for having said, "The majority of people die at thirty-five, but aren't buried until seventy-five." *Ouch!*

They're right. If people don't continue to grow, their hopes and dreams die. Life stagnates, and like those living with The Battered Career Syndrome® and The Battered Investor Syndrome®, people fall into a rut of perpetual disappointment and despair.

But that's not going to be the case for you. You're reading this book for a reason. You believe (or at least hope) something more is available to you beyond your current circumstances.

If you are not content with your current job or place in life, please don't feel shame or guilt about that dissatisfaction. The truth is, you're not alone. Nearly three-quarters of workers are actively thinking about quitting their job according to a survey cited in *Business Insider*.[1]

Even if it isn't vocational discontent that prompted you to pick up this book, we're glad you're reading it because it shows you're curious. And curiosity is often linked to intelligence.

In her coauthored article, *The Hungry Mind: Intellectual Curiosity Is the Third Pillar of Academic Performance*, Sophie von Stumm from the University of Edinburgh notes that "Curiosity is basically a hunger for exploration."[2] One study showed a direct correlation between that hunger and achievement. Researchers performed a meta-analysis, gathering data from approximately 200 studies totaling about 50,000 students. They found that curiosity did, indeed, influence academic performance.[3] In short, Einstein's famous saying, "Curiosity is more important than intelligence," proves true.

The bottom line is that you're in the right spot. You're willing to wonder. You're bold enough to ask whether there's something more in store for you and your future.

We've written this book with you in mind. Our goal isn't to convince you of anything. You're the only one who can choose what's right for you. We would be honored, however, to be your guides in this quest for discovery—*to explore what's possible.*

Unlock the Golden Handcuffs

The world shifted dramatically in the previous decade. The speed of technology and recent global events have produced yet another incredible rate of change in just the past twenty-four months. It would be imprudent to turn a blind eye to these events and assume everyone and everything has stayed the same—or to hope that life will simply return to "normal."

The result of all this change is that many people are reconsidering their context and careers. They are willing to ask tough questions, such as *Who am I? Why do I do what I do? Who am I doing it for?*

Gone are the days when people stayed at the same company for forty years and retired with a gold watch and an attractive pension plan. Characteristic of former generations, that career path often came with something else golden: handcuffs. As people reflect on what's important to them, they're waking up to the reality that a life sentence in day-job prison isn't worth giving up their freedom, finances, and the chance for fulfillment. They want *more.*

Maybe this is why we're seeing a career revolution. Think about it.

When was the last time you felt inspired or empowered? If you're like a lot of people, it's been a while—perhaps since childhood. The possibilities were endless when you were young. You could do anything. You dared to dream because failure wasn't an option or concern. You had the ability to focus on the end goal rather than all the obstacles you might encounter. Guess what? By tapping into your curiosity, you can reclaim your innate ability to dream and then use that power to reimagine your life and create your new future.

Sound too good to be true? It's not. Let's begin, and you'll see for yourself.

PART 1

REVOLT

CHAPTER 1

WELCOME TO THE CAREER REVOLUTION

You can cling to the present or create a new future.

It's not hard to make decisions
when you know what your values are.
—Roy Disney

Today's job market is nothing like the one previous generations experienced. Back then, most people worked for the same company for thirty or forty years. They counted on the security of a paycheck, benefits, and a pension plan that afforded them a similar standard of living to what they had before retirement.

This reality no longer exists.

The Career Revolution began with the loss of job security. Layoffs are the norm every time the economy down-shifts. While some jobs disappear as a result of technological advancements, others move to countries where labor is cheap and overhead costs are low. It's common for entire industries to move overseas—and take their jobs with them.

All of these changes have created a movement from job security to job insecurity. People today worry about the future of the marketplace—as well as their place in it:

- Will manufacturing increase domestically?
- Will jobs return?
- Will new ones be created? And if so, at what rate?
- And even if new jobs become available, would they be worth taking?

For most people, today's jobs are just a paycheck—one that may (or may not) cover the necessities. At best, jobs are a way to survive and pay the bills. Seven out of ten Americans live paycheck to paycheck.[4] Making matters worse, employees are often left struggling to manage hard-to-fund, self-directed retirement accounts. No wonder so many people feel like they're working hard and getting nowhere.

Many people think, *A job will do for now, but I need to figure out a way to save more money.* But can you save your way to prosperity and wealth?

Others think, *At least I have equity in my home.* Hopefully, this is the case for you, but for many, even that security has disappeared. Regardless, the question is: can equity in your home pave the way to independence and self-sufficiency? Perhaps, but only if that equity is leveraged and invested in something that has the potential to generate an ROI that creates cash flow. In the past, people based their career decisions, education, commitments, and goals on an abiding sense of security. But today, savings are down and stress has never been higher.

Much of the older generation has been displaced, and many feel a growing concern about their futures. They worry that ageism will lock them out of the marketplace.[5] Those who can secure jobs often find that their pay fails to keep pace with rising inflation rates.

On the other end of the age spectrum, young employees are entering a market unlike anything that has existed before. It is said that Gen Zers will have eighteen jobs spanning six careers in their lifetimes. Many of those jobs have nothing to do with the degrees that they earned at the expense of huge college loans—loans that will burden them with debt for decades.

To add to the sense of unpredictability and lack of control that today's employees feel, regardless of their age, is the diminished value of their retirement portfolios. Watching hard-earned investments decline in value can create extreme levels of stress, even despair.

Dealing with all this uncertainty throws some people into a victim mentality. They feel paralyzed by fear.

Other people are propelled, emboldened, and empowered to create a new future. Maybe that's you, and you're thinking: *there has to be a better way to work and live.*

IS IT TIME FOR YOU TO REVOLT?

Every generation has a poet bold enough to speak the truth plainly. Robert Frost challenged his generation with a simple choice, "Two roads diverged in a wood, and I took the one less traveled by."[6]

Fast forward several decades and Morpheus challenged Neo with a different choice. "You take the blue pill, the story ends, you wake up in your bed and believe whatever you want to believe. You take the red pill, you stay in wonderland, and I show you how deep the rabbit hole goes."[7]

You also have a choice: You can remain status quo or you can revolt. You can either step up to the challenge or simply reject the call.

We get it. *Revolt* is a strong word.

It's aggressive and bold, invoking a call to action and demanding a response.

A revolt means to "rise in rebellion."[8] Isn't that what creating a new future is all about? Rebelling against your current reality. Sometimes the simple act of recognizing that things aren't going well is a comfort in and of itself—a way to feel progress has been made, even though the situation has not been rectified. In our world's current situation, the realization that the marketplace has changed makes some people less likely to fall back on the illusion of security. Sure, some people hold out hope the economy might one day return to what it once was, but with every year that passes, fewer people are counting on things to return to "normal."

You owe it to yourself and your family to explore the options associated with taking ownership of your career and becoming financially self-sufficient. How would it make you feel if you knew you didn't have to worry about keeping a job to generate income? How would it make you feel to know you didn't have to check with a boss on where and when you need to show up for work? What if you knew that with every day that passes, your wealth and equity were growing and that you were self-reliant? That is what being self-sufficient is about. And when you equip yourself with the right information and apply your knowledge in a way you have never done before, you can experience a life you've never imagined.

Consider everything you've experienced up until this point in your life—including past hurts—as research and development that you can apply to your new future.

BATTERED CAREER SYNDROME° AND BATTERED INVESTOR SYNDROME°

In *Your Career 2.0*, we identified two painful situations that we call Battered Career Syndrome and Battered Investor Syndrome. See if you can relate.

Have you ever been in an unhappy job situation and while you've acknowledged that fact, you were unable to escape? Perhaps you admitted to the problem, but feeling trapped, put off trying to fix it. Or maybe you thought if you gave the role, your boss, this company, or perhaps another company another chance, things would be different?

Most employees understand things have changed, but their behavior patterns, which are based on habits they developed through years of working within the corporate system, remain on autopilot. They know there's a problem, but they're too accustomed to or fearful of removing themselves from the situation.

This mindset bears some resemblance to that of a battered spouse. Being involved in an abusive relationship is a serious situation, and in no way are we making light of it. The fact is, however, there are many parallels between the abused and the abuser and employees and the employers.

Employees often realize something is wrong while remaining caught in the cycle of behavior that keeps them entangled. It's not always a conscious choice, but simply the state of affairs to which they have become accustomed.

Seeing their friends get fired, receiving double the workload for less pay, and watching as their benefits get whittled away has become commonplace. The dreams and ideals these employees had when they took the job seem more and more distant. Unable to see an alternative, they stick with it even as the situation deteriorates. They're suffering from what we call the Battered Career Syndrome.

Take Paul, for example, a sales executive who has spent his entire career within the structure of a traditional job. His education and experience have enabled him to climb the ranks of the executive suite. He has spent his time putting in long hours, traveling for weeks on end, and missing out on events with his family and friends. He honestly believes he has to put up with these conditions to procure a steady income.

Now that Paul has reached the executive level, he continues to deal with his unsatisfying job in hopes that things will improve, or at least result in a better paycheck. Each day he returns to work, anticipating that things will be better, only to find that he's repeating the cycle over and over again. He's going nowhere and doesn't have the first clue about how to escape the situation. Other alternatives like self-employment seem too frightening, and he has no idea what other options might exist. Paul is a classic example of someone suffering from Battered Career Syndrome.

Much like a battered spouse, employees like Paul are too scared to leave untenable situations. Facing an unknown future without a plan, these employees continue in the same cycle because they believe there will be a paycheck, even if they don't have an ideal work environment or career. They can't imagine an alternative and believe that if they stay, somehow things will get better.

It's only when the urge to protect themselves and their families trumps their fears, that they finally venture beyond the traditional employee mindset. Their life-changing moment comes when they take that first step and do something different. It may take all the courage they can muster at the time, but one day they look back and realize that moment of change was not nearly as frightening as the situation they left. The experience is similar for victims of Battered Investors Syndrome. Because of the rapid changes in the market, many investors walk around dazed and confused, feeling beaten down and uncertain about what just happened, *again*. Since many investors are passive investors, they don't feel like they have control and feel victimized by the highs and lows of the economy, the stock market, inflation, interest rates, etc.

Many people find it hard to escape the Battered Career or the Battered Investors syndrome, and as a result, they continue to exist within a **cycle of insanity—repeating the same actions over and over again but expecting different results.** Breaking free from either of these scenarios requires a fundamental shift in the way people think about their careers and investments.

IT'S TIME FOR A WAKE-UP CALL.

Maybe your situation isn't as dire as someone suffering from the Battered Career or Battered Investors Syndrome. Perhaps you have come to the realization that a corporate job or traditional investments are unlikely to enable you to reach your goals of being self-sufficient, experiencing financial freedom, or building long-term wealth and equity. If that's the case, you're primed for a career revolution.

That's great news. Change is on the horizon! But because change can feel scary and fear has a way of pushing people back into the familiarity of unhealthy, unfulfilling, and unprofitable situations, we want to make sure you understand the consequences of *not* making a change. Before charging ahead, let's unpack what employees give up without even realizing it.

THE TRADE-OFFS

Consider whether you have done any of these things as an employee:

- spent too much time commuting or traveling
- worn your eyes out staring at the screen for hours on end in unproductive videoconferencing
- relocated from one city to the next to appease your company

- felt guilty about missing your children's events in the name of keeping up with your vocational responsibilities
- regretted not spending enough time with your family

In today's financial environment, it has become nearly impossible to earn an income, maintain a healthy lifestyle, and build a nest egg without sacrificing nearly all of your time to the job.

Time with your family is not the only trade-off you are making, however. You are also foregoing the opportunity to follow your dreams. Today, people often work fifty, sixty, or even seventy hours a week just to keep up. That's time and energy spent building someone else's dream and contributing to their Income, Lifestyle, Wealth, and Equity—not yours or your family's.

An article on the popular blog *20 Something Finance,* titled "The U.S. is the Most Overworked Developed Nation in the World," highlights data that reveal America's unhealthy obsession with work. Compared to many other first-world countries, our employees put in more hours and get less paid time off. Productivity in the United States has increased 430 percent since 1950 as worker hours have continually increased. So, what is the byproduct of all this effort and time? Unfortunately, it is usually to build someone else's wealth. Whether we want to admit it or not, that's essentially what most employees are doing today.[9]

This realization can create a lot of frustration. But just for a moment, set all that frustration aside and imagine a different future.

- What would happen if you started spending all those hours doing something for yourself?
- What would your life look like?
- What would you do if failure were not an option?

As you answer these questions, you will begin to see possibilities. That's when frustration turns into fascination. You will also start to realize that uncertainty is often where the opportunity lies.

So how do you turn that growing awareness of possibility into a tangible goal?

TURNING SAND INTO PEARLS

Our company's research shows that 75 percent of all adults are searching for something other than a job.[10] They have a sense that better options—a different path from the rat race—exist. But in their quest for self-sufficiency and financial independence, they experience constant frustration.

If you can relate and are dissatisfied with the traditional job market or your current investment portfolio, think of that discontent as a grain of sand inside an oyster. The persistent irritation isn't necessarily a bad thing. An oyster turns an irritating piece of sand into a precious pearl. In terms of your career, the constant irritation produced by the frustration about the job market or your passive investments motivates you to look outside of what you know and allows you to see greater possibilities for your future.

The truth is that the economy and the job market are never going to be what they once were. Things are always changing. We have entered a completely different world. Looking the other way and denying the reality of the situation is not an option. Acknowledging these facts is the catalyst for transformation. By accepting and *addressing* reality, you have the power to turn your grain of sand into a pearl.

POSSIBILITIES, OPTIONS, AND DREAMS

By now you might be wondering whether there is any bright spot in all of this seemingly hopeless reality. The answer is a resounding, *yes!* Your next step begins with tuning into your possibilities, options, and dreams. They're within your grasp. To create the empowerment needed to reach them, you must first transform your mindset.

Developing a new mindset is like training your body to reach and maintain a healthy weight. Everyone knows that eating a healthful diet and getting the proper amount of exercise are necessary for a healthy body. It's a simple formula. Empowering someone to change the way they eat and exercise is far less simple. Giving up on the desired result in the short term is almost always easier than developing the habits that will ultimately result in what people say they want.

Similarly, you may be able to see new possibilities for your life and career. And you know that to achieve what you desire will require you to change the way you look at your career and the road to greater Income, Lifestyle, Wealth, and Equity. That is easier said than done. But with the right tools and the motivation to follow through on your goals, your career dreams *can* become a reality.

The late motivational speaker Brian Klemmer wrote a book titled *If How-To's Were Enough, we would all be Skinny, Rich, and Happy.* In it, he suggested that humans need more than information to increase the likelihood of success. They need direction, ongoing support, and accountability. People who work with a nutritionist or a physical trainer are more likely to achieve their desired weight or fitness goals. Those professionals keep people focused and moving toward their goals. The same is true for those who work with a Career Ownership Coach.

Since we know the old options are unreliable, the question is this: *How will you take control of your financial future to get from where you are to where you want to be?* This may be a major transition for you, and fear of the unknown can be a powerful obstacle, even when you know you are moving toward something better—something more secure and within your control.

MAKE THE SWITCH

The traditional corporate job has always required a time-and-effort based mindset, meaning you get compensated for the time and effort you put in, not necessarily for the results you produce. To even imagine the possibility of focusing on the results that come with taking personal responsibility like that of self-employment can be a difficult and scary transition.

Historically, employees have been able to exist in a time-and-effort economy regardless of whether they were in a position directly responsible for producing results. Many feel like they are just a cog in the system, and that can be frustrating. In contrast, entrepreneurs, investors, and business owners have always depended solely on their results.

Knowing that you are responsible for your results and income can be a crippling or empowering revelation. The reality is that even if you have a job, you aren't guaranteed a life of ease. The perceived security the corporate world offers has proved unreliable. Education and experience no longer ensure a secure job, and the stock market fluctuates wildly, even on the best of days.

But what if you could find a way where you don't have to trade time for money? What if you could participate in the results economy rather than the time-and-effort economy? Can you imagine how your life and lifestyle might improve?

If you're ready to make the switch from a job based on time and effort (or are curious about that possibility), one thing you'll need to remember is that the formula that got you to your current situation will not be the one that can help you reach your vision of a more prosperous future. In other words, you've got to let go of the past and move toward your future.

Notice that I didn't say you should forget your past. You must, in fact, reflect on the winning formulas from your past. The places where you've been and the experiences you've collected may not have led to the perfect corporate job, but they could very well lead to other successes in your life. Use what you've learned along the way as a basis for greater confidence in switching to more proactive career and investment vehicles.

BREAK FREE FROM WHAT'S HOLDING YOU BACK

Would you like to steer your own ship? Or at the very least, take full ownership and control of your career?

Most people say they would—but it's amazing how few actually do it. Perhaps that's because taking ownership requires a significantly higher level of personal responsibility.

Making the switch starts with gathering facts and information and exploring new territories. The simplest, most direct route to controlling your destiny and financial future is by observing how others do it; and then determining what your options are for doing the same.

The biggest mistake most people make when it comes to working on their Income, Lifestyle, Wealth, and Equity goals is failing to learn about the options they have to achieve them. Educating yourself requires taking personal responsibility for your future, and it's the only way to discover what is possible.

For many people, taking control usually means reaching self-sufficiency through career ownership. This can be a scary move if you are stuck in the mindset that having a job is the less risky path. And let's be honest, it's tempting to immediately dismiss possibilities that lie outside your current comfort zone. Thomas Jefferson understood this tendency to seek the familiar and offered an alternative course of action: "If you want something you've never had, you must be willing to do something you've never done."[11]

There are many reasons why people don't seriously and intentionally explore all their options. In our experience, the main reason is that people don't know where to start. They're terrified of striking out into the unknown all by themselves. And, unfortunately, the fear of failure is often stronger than their desire for success.

Don't fall into that trap. Don't let fear win.

If you find yourself jumping to conclusions right now, thinking, *okay, I know what this is about; his is never going to work for me,* please don't limit your options. Keep an open mind. Consider possibilities, gather the information, and do the research. As you educate yourself on your options, you'll heighten your awareness and open your mind to explore and discover. Doing so will help you look at the facts instead of reacting to preconceived notions and emotions.

If you are willing to explore the possibilities, we'll guide you through a Journey of Discovery™. It's your way out and it will help you break free from your current reality—the corporate chains and the self-imposed mental limitations.

Ninety-five percent of the people who have gone through this Journey of Discovery say that they ended up discovering options they would have never considered before or would have prematurely dismissed.[12]

We helped them not rush to conclusions prematurely. We reassured them that, if upon gathering the facts they validate their first reaction was on target, then they have a new perspective with which they can go back to the job market or whatever else they were doing.

They will no longer feel that irritation, that grain of sand, they felt before because they have taken the time to think about their thinking.

We encourage you to do the same and to remain open. We're not asking you to make any decisions prematurely. In fact, we won't ask you to make any decisions at all. Once you gather the facts, you'll reach a point of clarity and the best next step will be evident.

So, take a chance. Go ahead and explore this world of possibilities with the kind of childlike wonder that refused to be limited or diminished by the fear of failure. The possibilities you discover just may lead you to your dreams.

In the next chapter, we'll help you start writing your own success story—your You 2.0®. If your current path, career, life, and success can be considered You 1.0, imagine what an even better version of your career, life, and success could look like. In essence, you, only better: You 2.0. But first, please take the brief POD, the Possibilities, Options, and Dreams Assessment© to see whether you are living your best life and tapping into your possibilities, options, and dreams.

Access the online version here:

POD Assessment Instructions

This is a fun, enlightening exercise that requires less than five minutes of your time. After completing the POD Assessment©, you'll discover your POD score.

Read the following statements. Choose the answer that best represents the way you think and feel about the past thirty days. Go with your gut, your first inclination. There is no right or wrong answer. And the more honest you are, the more empowering this journey will be.

Possibilities

1. My life is fluid and full of new adventures.
   Never | Almost Never | Often | Almost Always | Always

2. I feel like I am in control of my destiny.
   Never | Almost Never | Often | Almost Always | Always

3. I am free to spend time doing the things that matter most.
   Never | Almost Never | Often | Almost Always | Always

Options

4. I can make a difference and achieve my personal and professional goals.
   Never | Almost Never | Often | Almost Always | Always

5. I am willing to explore new people, places, and ideas.
   Never | Almost Never | Often | Almost Always | Always

6. I believe in rewriting the rules in life and business.
   Never | Almost Never | Often | Almost Always | Always

Dreams

7. I am insanely curious about new things in life and business.
Never | Almost Never | Often | Almost Always | Always

8. I imagine a bigger and brighter future.
Never | Almost Never | Often | Almost Always | Always

9. I envision a life where I am truly self-sufficient.
Never | Almost Never | Often | Almost Always | Always

10. I can imagine myself in three years living the life of my dreams.
Never | Almost Never | Often | Almost Always | Always

POD Assessment Scoring

Review the ten questions above and count up how many fit each of the five categories and write that number in the respective blank below:

Never: _____ x (1) =
Almost Never: _____ x (2) =
Often: _____ x (3) =
Almost Always: _____ x (4) =
Always: _____ x (5) =

TOTAL

Multiply each number you wrote in each blank by the number to the right in parentheses.

POD ASSESSMENT KEY

Total all five numbers from the evaluation above and reference the Flow Trigger Key below.

1–10: My life contains little to no possibilities, options, or dreams. I am not living my best life and I don't feel satisfied.

11–20: I have experienced possibilities and options and have pursued my dreams a few times. When I did, I felt great, but my life doesn't contain enough of these components to produce joy, peace, and purpose regularly.

21–30: I experience possibilities and options or reach for my dreams about half of the time. When I do, I feel amazing and inspired. The other 50 percent of the time, however, I feel a sense of discontent with my work or life.

31–40: I often experience possibilities and options. I follow my dreams. Since my life contains these components regularly, I feel incredibly fulfilled.

41–50: My life is organized around new possibilities, exploring options, and living my dreams. I experience these components daily, and because of this, I am living my best life.

CHAPTER 2

WRITE YOUR OWN SUCCESS STORY

There's a You 2.0® ready to be unleashed.

I have one life and one chance
to make it count for something.
I'm free to choose what that something is.

—Jimmy Carter

Success doesn't look the same for everyone. Therefore, one of the most important objectives of your Journey of Discovery is to gain clarity toward answering these questions:

1. What does success look like for you?
2. What do you need to do and who do you need to become to experience it?
3. What does your You 2.0 look like?

There is no right or wrong answer. What is best for you will be unique and depend on many factors, such as your age, dreams, personality, financial position, family obligations, and experience. It often helps to think in terms of:

- What are my Income goals, needs, and expectations?
- What are my Lifestyle goals, needs, and expectations?
- Longer term, what are my Wealth and Equity goals, needs, and expectations?

Throughout this book, we'll share relatable examples of five people—Kevin, John, Beth, Doug, and Emily—who are on their journey of discovery, evaluating new possibilities for their lives. They are composites of real-life clients, people just like you, who want more out of life. They are also coming to this experience from different perspectives and with different needs, so just as it will be for you, success for each of them looks different as well.

For example, Kevin is fifty years old. From the outside looking in, it seems as if he has everything going for him. He has a wonderful wife and three kids who will be heading to college soon. He has a great career and a high-paying job. So, what's missing? Kevin is tired of feeling like he has no control. He is tired of being forced to work so hard for a paycheck but no equity. Ultimately, he feels like he is working on someone else's dream and not his own.

On the contrary, John has had a good career and is nearing retirement age and suddenly finds that his Social Security benefits and pension won't go as far as he had expected. To travel with his wife the way he has always dreamed of, and to keep his current lifestyle, he will need to explore some additional income streams.

Beth, who is only at the midpoint of her career (even though she is an executive and a force to be reckoned with), isn't happy with the rigid structure of her current corporate environment. She yearns for more flexibility, more free time, and less travel but needs to keep her income at least at the level it is right now.

And Doug is in his late twenties. He was hoping for a steady job after he got his degree in business, but he's already had to change jobs three times due to no fault of his own. Mergers. Acquisitions. The elimination of jobs. He feels like he is already behind, even though he has just begun. He was looking forward to paying off his college loans, eliminating some debt, and saving a little before proposing to his girlfriend. Things are simply not happening the way he had planned for.

And how about thirty-year-old Emily, a single mom with two kids? She wants to start saving for their college educations, while still having time to help them with their homework. She feels like she is working hard and going fast but not making progress fast enough. At this rate, she wonders if she will *ever* have enough money saved up for her kids' education.

All five of these people want greater Income, Lifestyle, Wealth, and Equity. The specifics of their goals for the future, their success stories, and the paths they take to get there will differ dramatically.

Creating your success story and a vision for your life begins with a paradigm shift where you can start seeing yourself and your aspirations as the greatest proactive tools in your arsenal. Such a shift in thinking creates a multiplier effect, which allows you to get significantly greater results with less time, energy, and effort.

You've heard the saying, "What got you here won't get you there." This aphorism is especially relevant to taking ownership and personal responsibility for your career. You need to scrutinize your actions. You must ask yourself:

Do you tend to take the path of least resistance and avoid reflecting on your thoughts and actions?

- Do you take responsibility for your life and future?
- Do you close yourself to possibilities just because you never considered them before?
- Are you afraid of change?

A complete rethink of what a *career* means is needed when you write your success story in today's world. Each iteration of humankind has had to do so.

In the early days, survival required people to hunt for and gather food. As time passed, we started to farm. We created ways to harvest what we sowed and were able to acquire food with reasonable predictability. Then came the Industrial Revolution and with it, the creation of jobs—the kind of jobs that many are now still hoping for today, where there is a vast dependency on the employer. Although we have long since entered the Digital Revolution that—along with economic challenges and globalization—has ignited the Career Revolution.

The Journey of Discovery is a powerful experience we take together. It holds up a mirror to help you see the life you want to live and then shines a light on the available options that can help you achieve that life. When people first engage with a Career Ownership Coach, they often are looking for material things outside themselves: better opportunities, the perfect job, or the latest investment, business, or franchise opportunity. The purpose of this journey is to help you look within. Yes, it may seem counterintuitive because it seems like the perfect solution must lie outside of you, but that is not so. First, you need to take a look within to envision the future you desire by defining your Income, Lifestyle, Wealth, and Equity goals, needs, and expectations, and only then does it help to start learning about ways to accomplish those.

A critical component of this journey is the safe space it provides for you to explore your options and figure out what you want and what works best for you. After all, you're the you want and what works best for you. After all, you're the only one who can define *your* success. We have created an experience for you to educate yourself, learn, discover, and become aware of what is possible. Changing your mindset and redefining your career path can feel overwhelming, but using the possibilities, options, and dreams approach will empower you, no matter what direction you end up choosing as it relates to your future.

It's easy to think that you don't deserve or aren't worthy of this safe space because of your background or past failures—or because you've had life easy compared to some and should just be content with what you have. Or maybe you believe you have to be the tough person—the one who takes on others' burdens but never thinks to ask for help. Don't let your self-doubt, fear, or pride stand in the way of exploring your options in a truly safe environment. Remember: You don't have to jump off any cliffs. The goal of the Journey of Discovery is to look at all the options with clear eyes so you can get a better sense of what is possible.

INCOME, LIFESTYLE, WEALTH, AND EQUITY (I.L.W.E.*)

As you begin to define your goals, needs, and expectations, it helps to relate them to four basic concepts:

1. Income
2. Lifestyle
3. Wealth
4. Equity

We have used these terms previously as a way of pinpointing some tangible goals, needs, and expectations for the future. They are all directly affected by your professional career. Let's take a moment to define goals, needs, and expectations before we look at how each relates to the four important Income, Lifestyle, Wealth, and Equity (I.L.W.E.) terms. With that foundation, you'll be able to determine what direction you want your future to take.

GOALS

A goal is an idea of the future or desired result that a person or a group of people envision, plan, and commit to achieving.[13] People endeavor to reach goals within a finite time by setting deadlines.

A goal is roughly similar to a purpose or aim. The anticipated result or end guides one's actions. It might be a physical object or an abstract object that has intrinsic value.

As it relates to the Journey of Discovery, a goal is a benefit or a result you desire in the future.

NEEDS

Needs are distinguished from wants in that the deficiency of a need causes a clear adverse outcome: a dysfunction or even death. In other words, a need is something required for a safe, stable, and healthy life (e.g., air, water, food, land, and shelter).[14] In contrast, a want is a desire, wish, or aspiration.

As it relates to what we are talking about, a need is a non-negotiable benefit or result you must have. It is hard or maybe impossible to strive for a goal when your basic needs aren't being met.

EXPECTATIONS

An expectation is what is considered the most likely to happen. An expectation, which is a belief about something that will occur in the future, may or may not be realistic. When your expectations are not met, you may feel disappointment. If something happens that is not at all expected, you may feel surprised. Anticipation is the emotion you feel regarding an expectation.

As it relates to what we are discussing, expectations are reasonable assumptions about the results of the change and the possibilities you are seeking.

Now let's look at how your goals, needs, and expectations relate to Income, Lifestyle, Wealth, and Equity.

INCOME

Income is typically a shorter-term goal. You can see its effects immediately—with large, regular deposits of money and growing bank account balances. While this term seems fairly straightforward, in reality, the concept of income and what each of us wants out of it has changed drastically.

Where once the people who started on the Journey of Discovery wanted to double or even triple their incomes, now many are simply trying to maintain the same level of income they once had. If they've lost their jobs, getting another one at the previous salary has become increasingly difficult as jobs are disappearing or are being filled by younger employees who are willing to accept a smaller paycheck.

For generations, people became accustomed to having their careers and incomes grow consistently between the ages of thirty-five and fifty, but this is no longer a given for most people. Income expectations are being upended, and many employees have come to realize that they traded off time with their families for a paycheck that no longer exists. As a result, goals, needs, and expectations revolving around income have become more about finding security outside the corporate world during a time when real income is declining, starting salaries are decreasing, and long-term unemployment for those fifty-five and older is growing exponentially.

LIFESTYLE

Lifestyle is another shorter-term goal with immediately visible effects. We often hear clients say they've been working sixty-hour weeks and now want to earn a dependable living while being able to fully live their lives. They want the freedom and flexibility to attend their kids' soccer games or enjoy romantic dinners with their spouses or simply have the freedom and flexibility to work from wherever they want to. In previous years, everything revolved around earning a bigger income. Now, their focus has shifted to earning the same level of income outside the rat race of the traditional workplace. These people are not afraid to work, and they know they still have to put in the hours; they just want to do it in a way that better molds their careers around their lifestyles.

The corporate world had many of us convinced the best way to give our families a prosperous lifestyle was with trade-offs. Whether the company matched our retirement plan or even offered pension plans. In the past, many counted on their pension plans only to find out that pension plans aren't necessarily a guarantee as many plans are underfunded or can even terminate.[15] Nowadays, most jobs no longer offer pension plans. Only 56 percent of employers in the US offer a 401K plan and only half of them offer an employer match.[16, 17] Devoting yourself entirely to your job was supposed to guarantee you would one day achieve your lifestyle goals. More often than not, that expectation has resulted in disappointment.

WEALTH

Income comes before wealth. Once you develop income, you create a lifestyle that suits you. The right opportunity will allow you to do both. Income and lifestyle are immediate concerns. Wealth, however, is a more long-term concern. Building wealth requires taking your increasing income and growing it even larger as you prepare for the future. This is done through investing, diversifying income streams, and purchasing assets with wealth-building elements to them.

EQUITY

The final piece of the puzzle is equity, the strategy you develop once you have all your assets in place. Equity is your ownership of any asset after all debts associated with that asset are paid off. For example, a car or house with no outstanding debt is considered the owner's equity because he or she can readily sell the item for cash. Stocks are equity because they represent ownership in a corporation. When you choose to own a business as a way to create self-sufficiency and financial independence, you are building equity as you pay off the debts associated with the business.

Use the Personal Income, Lifestyle, Wealth, and Equity Worksheet to help get your mind going and start dreaming. Just one rule: This is not the time to justify or rationalize. Allow yourself to dream big! Later, we will help you figure out what you will need to do to turn your dream into reality.

*"If you never dream, you will
never know the endless possibilities
of what you can become."*
—Annette White

Access the digital worksheet here:

Personal Income, Lifestyle, Wealth, and Equity Worksheet

Component	In 6 Months	In 12 Months	In 5 Years	In 10 Years+
Income:				
Annual Income				
Investment Income				
Other Income				
Lifestyle:				
Family and Relationships				
Hobbies and Pastimes				
Travel and Leisure				
Time to volunteer				
Education and Personal Development				
Major Purchases				
Other:				
Wealth:				
Investments				
Retirement				
Professional Growth				
Other:				
Equity:				
Property:				
Other:				
Other:				
Other:				

TAKE BACK CONTROL OF YOUR LIFE

The problem we encounter today is that many people we work with no longer believe that wealth and equity can grow in today's world. Some trends suggest that on average, millennials are worse off financially compared to the Boomers and Gen Xers at their same age due to trying to enter the job market after the great recession and increased debt due to student loans. Not exactly a heartwarming trend. What will it be like for the Gen Zers?

Back in the heyday of corporations, people spent a great deal of time thinking about and planning for their future; now that the reset button has been hit, all bets are off. As a result, many believe they must jettison their expectations and settle for less today and in the future, and, unfortunately, that's the example they're setting for their children.

Young people are witnessing the struggle and heartbreak their parents go through in the traditional job system. This is a problem because it sets up the next generation for disappointment. The Swiss psychologist Carl Jung asked the question, "What's the most damaging thing in the life of a child?" In all of his research, he determined the "unlived life of the parent" had the most detrimental impact on a child.[18]

We owe it to our children to show them that they can take control of their lives and careers. That it is possible to set goals and grow the Income, Lifestyle, Wealth, and Equity they want. We need to show them how to be ready to change and to adapt when the situation requires it. Most importantly, we need to be an example of how to be open to different possibilities.

Wealth and equity have become enigmas. In most cases, people are just happy to get back to some semblance of what used to be normal. Expectations may be lower, but it's the mindset they've adopted to survive the career shift. Dwelling on the reality of the situation is too painful and too embarrassing.

Most people aren't even conscious of the fact that they've given up on their dreams. Settling has become the new normal. The good news is that we have a choice: We get to choose if and how we shape our future and create a legacy.

ARE YOU SETTLING?

Consider how each person in the following scenarios is settling. Which, if any, of them do you relate to most?

In our five earlier cases:

1. **Kevin**: The fifty-year-old, who seems like he has everything going for him. He has a great family. He has a great career and a high-paying job. So, what's missing? Kevin is tired of feeling as if he has no con- trol. He is tired of being forced to work so hard for a paycheck but no equity. Ultimately, he feels like he is working on someone else's dream and not his own. As he is thinking and talking to family and friends, he is starting to wonder about the reason for his dissatis- faction and restlessness. Could he be going through a midlife crisis? Would it be stupid and reckless to change course at this point in his career? Would he be letting down those who rely on him? What if he piv- ots and ends up worse off than before? Perhaps if he just hunkers down and immerses himself deeper into his job, he'll forget about the discontent that has been nagging at him.

2. **John**: The near retiree decides that he and his wife can't travel as they had dreamed of doing when they retired. They must live within their means after John retires, knowing his pension will barely cover their bills.

3. **Beth**: Despite her rigid work schedule, Beth has resigned herself to staying in her current job because

32

she believes that finding a new one in her industry will be impossible.

4. **Doug:** He puts off proposing to his girlfriend out of concern for his lingering college debts.

5. **Emily:** She realizes if she wants her children to have a good college education, she'll have to sacrifice spending time with them to work the longer hours needed to get the high-paying promotion.

Each of these people feels they have to compromise or give up their dreams and settle for whatever meager handouts the corporate world is willing to offer them. These outcomes, however, don't have to be a foregone conclusion.

Kevin, John, Beth, Doug, and Emily can choose to write a different story. They can take control of their lives and ownership of their careers. So can you. By educating yourself, learning about your options, especially if they are out of your current comfort zone, and defining your goals and dreams, you can empower yourself to build the level of Income, Lifestyle, Wealth, and Equity you desire.

Think of your dreams like a silver tea set given to you by your grandparents. Wanting to protect this treasure and afraid it may get broken, you hide it away in the china cabinet and then forget you even have it. As time passes, you assume it's lost until one day you find it by accident. It may be heavily tarnished, but once you polish it, you realize you still have a wonderful treasure. Your dreams are your treasures. They will guide you to the actions required to achieve them, but first, you need to rediscover and clarify them.

THE BIG QUESTIONS

To clarify your dreams, you need to look deep inside. You need to take that tea set out and inspect it closely. Let's begin by asking some big questions to help you paint an exact picture of the future you want.

First Question: *How would you describe your feelings about your present career?*

More often than not, the answer to this question is simply frustration. Long hours, less pay, and no security for the future combine to create a sense of dissatisfaction that eventually becomes too irritating to ignore, like that grain of sand we mentioned earlier.

Take time to think about this question. Don't just use one word to answer it. Instead, describe how it makes you feel. It's natural to avoid things that feel uncomfortable or that produce pain. Now is not the time to do that. The goal is to become completely aware of exactly the way your current situation makes you feel.

Second Question: *What do you want more of in your life, personally and professionally? And conversely, what do you want less of?*

Maybe you want more income and more free time, as many of our clients do. But this is your time to dream and you're the one clarifying your dreams, so don't limit yourself. For example, at a personal level, you may want to travel more, learn another language, be present at your children's functions and sporting events, or volunteer. In your career, you may seek more personal fulfillment, or perhaps spend less time dealing with your boss' whims or your subordinates' drama.

These two questions help you home in on exactly the kind of lifestyle you want and bring clarity to the career path that will work best for you.

With these first questions answered, more detailed introspection can begin.

- Five years from now, if you stay on your current career path, how do you see your options?
- How do you see yourself achieving financial independence?
- What are your biggest concerns about changing careers?
- If you knew you couldn't fail, what career would you choose?

These kinds of questions immediately generate strong emotions, and emotions can be powerful motivators that empower you to make a change. You may find that they also elicit an almost visceral response that helps you create a detailed picture of the life and career you want. The goal is to create a clear picture of your dreams.

YOU 2.0®

Consider the following question: If we looked at your life a year from today, what has to have happened during that period, both personally and professionally, for you to be happy with your progress?

This question is inspired by Dan Sullivan. He refers to it as the R-Factor Question. R stands for relationship. Building a relationship and building trust are essential to being able to empower people to go from where they are today to where they aspire to be in the future. The R-Factor Question is also known as the Dan Sullivan Question.[19]

Creating the new version of yourself—your YOU 2.0®— requires you to identify the following three aspects of your life: your dangers, opportunities, and strengths. Once you know what they are, the next step is to set a goal that excites you and gives you focus. Defining goals around your dangers, opportunities, and strengths will assist you in dealing with or taking advantage of these circumstances so you can achieve the Income, Lifestyle, Wealth, and Equity you desire.

DANGERS

Dangers are those things that keep you up at night. They are the obstacles and issues you may face right now or in the future. They worry you and make you feel that you have no options or control. They include:

- How much longer will you be employable?
- How much more limited will your career options get as time goes by?
- Is your age a limitation? Are you considered too old by employers? Will you ever get another job at your age?
- Can you afford to wait to take control of your destiny?
- Are your current skills transferable?
- Do you have any opportunities to build the wealth and equity you desire for yourself and your family?
- How will you be able to fund your longer and more active life expectancy? Will you end up depending on your children?
- Will the value of your investments and savings keep going down until you have nothing left for your retirement?
- How long will you be able to keep your current job? Will there be any other positions available if you lose your job?

What other probable or current circumstances create sleepless nights for you?

It's time to get proactive. You are not a victim of your circumstances. You have the power to take control of your life and change your destiny. In response to each of the dangers you identified from the questions above, create a goal that will empower you. How could you turn those obstacles into opportunities to *rescue* your dreams?

OPPORTUNITIES

Opportunities are circumstances or possibilities in your life that motivate you. These are the things that get you excited. Your life is filled with opportunities and possibilities. Sometimes, however, the obstacles in your life prevent you from seeing the many opportunities that surround you. Here are a few opportunities to focus on. Make a check mark by the ones that strike a chord:

- the ability to take control of your destiny
- your desire to spend more time on the things that matter most to you
- your dream to reach your desired Income, Lifestyle, Wealth, and Equity
- your commitment to one day be financially independent and experience true financial freedom
- your aspiration to mitigate your risks and fast-track your career
- your intention to create the lifestyle of your dreams
- your determination to fund your longer and more active life expectancy
- your curiosity to discover new possibilities beyond your current experiences
- your yearning to be re-energized and passionate about life and your career
- your longing to have the time and financial ability to give back to your community

What other opportunities excite you and make you want to change your circumstances?

It's time to leave behind the dread of paralyzing fear and revel in the hope that the new you—your YOU 2.0®—can bring into your life. It's time to focus on what you want and not on what keeps you in the past. For each of the opportunities that resonated with you, identify the actions you will have to take to transform them from longings to reality.

STRENGTHS

Strengths are your unique talents, capabilities, and skills that you can use to create the next version of yourself—YOU 2.0®. Your strengths become the tools you'll use to uncover the person that you need to be to achieve your dreams—your desired Income, Lifestyle, Wealth, and Equity.

It's easy to focus only on your weaknesses and fail to recognize your assets. It's even more important, however, to identify and acknowledge your strengths. Look at the list below and make a note of which ones apply to you:

- the success you have had in your current and previous jobs or careers
- good health, energy, and vitality
- a large circle of influence and a strong community of peers
- the ability to make good choices and go to work to make them good decisions
- an impeccable work ethic
- numerous transferable skills
- a long record of accomplishments
- a high degree of integrity
- a possibilities mindset

- a positive attitude
- a strong belief you can succeed at everything on which you focus your attention
- an ability to adapt and embrace change

What other strengths do you have that will help you become YOU 2.0® so you can achieve your dreams?

Once you've taken stock of your strengths, your next step is to strategize how you can use them to create the new you—YOU 2.0®. Describe how you plan to use each of the strengths you identified as an asset in your strategy. How will they help you write your success story?

If this feels like an impossible exercise, please know that most of our clients have felt the same way. What they have found, however, is that by working alongside a Career Ownership Coach, their dreams and the strategies for making them a reality come into focus. Their coaches help them identify blind spots and challenge their limiting beliefs. Before long, something that seemed overwhelming, possibly even insurmountable, turns into something they are excited about and inspired to pursue.

Now that you've asked all these questions and have created your goals, don't worry too much, if it feels more like a rough pencil sketch as opposed to a beautiful Rembrandt. Once again, create a picture in your mind of yourself a year from now, two years from now, and three years from now, living the life you've always wanted. Think of the steps that got you there. A key component of this experience is to get beyond your current circumstances. Set your mind free to give yourself permission to dream and envision the future you want.

After working with people just like you for almost forty years, we've created the YOU 2.0® Worksheet. The worksheet will take you through the process we have discussed here. We encourage you to access it online and work through it. If you do so, you'll discover that regardless of how dire or isolating your circumstances appear to be, you have opportunities and strengths that can help you achieve your dreams.

And remember: You are not alone. Hundreds of thousands, maybe even millions, of people today are dealing with similar issues.

Access the digital version here:

PART 2

REIMAGINE

CHAPTER 3

DISCOVER WHAT HOLDS
YOU BACK

Every obstacle is an opportunity in disguise.

*All those obstacles that seem to
oppose our goals are actually the raw
material for achieving them.*

—Dan Sullivan

Humans are interesting creatures. We're not always logical or rational. Consider the following example.

Dartmouth researchers asked study participants this simple question:

Suppose you were working and could choose between different kinds of jobs. Which would you prefer: being an employee or being self-employed?

The study determined that 70.8 percent of Americans want to be self-employed.[20]

Now contrast that figure, which equates to seven out of ten people, to the number of people who actually are self-employed. A Bureau of Labor Statistics report from 2022 found that roughly 9.9 million out of 164 million Americans are self-employed. That's only 6 percent of the population.

Why the drastic discrepancy between what people want and what people do?

Could it be because most of us have a strong to very strong desire to be self-sufficient but are scared to death of the personal responsibility and perceived risk of being self-employed?

If the road toward self-sufficiency and financial freedom were free of obstacles and challenges, almost everyone would take it. But the truth is, even exploring possibilities that are currently outside of your current comfort zone can be scary. The sheer magnitude of choices can feel overwhelming.

In addition to wading through the options, figuring out the difference between what you *really* want and what you initially *think* you want can be confusing. For example, you may think that because you need to make more money, you need a better job. But is making more money the ultimate goal? Or is finding the job the ultimate goal? Or is the goal to have the ability to keep more of your earnings to do the things you wish to do? What if you were to find out that small business owners can legally reduce their tax bills compared to W-2 employees and keep a greater percentage of their earnings? Would that change your goal in any way?

In this chapter, we're going to ask you to peel the layers to get to the heart of what you really want. Clarifying your true goal will help identify the best path forward.

We must warn you, however, that as you go through this time of soul-searching, you may experience a variety of emotions, obstacles, and concerns. Considering options outside the traditional job market will certainly lead you to contend with some *F-words*. And if you aren't mindful of their potential, the following common F-words can derail you:

1. Frustration
2. Fear

3. Financial Constraints
4. Family and Friends

The important thing to remember is that you can overcome all of these roadblocks—regardless of whether they are real or perceived—if you focus on the most important F-word of all: *financial freedom.* Let's unpack some of these F-Words a little more.

FRUSTRATION

Are you feeling under-appreciated?

How about feeling left out of important decisions or stymied by bureaucratic flab?

Are you in a dead-end job, waiting your turn for that pink slip?

Do you ever feel you could do great things if you could run the show?

Do you feel like you are working hard but have nothing to show for it?

These circumstances all lead to frustration.

When it comes to frustration, there are two kinds: healthy and unhealthy. The healthy type of frustration can motivate you to take action. It instills willpower and a purpose that drives you to achieve. It brings about an absolute resolve that you will not allow your current circumstances to determine your future.

It is easy to think of historical figures or even everyday heroes who reached deep within themselves and, despite the challenges they face, found the courage and the strength to do something remarkable with their lives. Many times, their resolve to overcome and succeed was born from frustration.

But then there's the unhealthy kind of frustration—the kind that can be demoralizing and paralyzing. People suffering from this type of frustration may feel as if a dark cloud looms over them, preventing them from taking control of their lives.

At some level, people suffering from unhealthy frustration find comfort in the state of frustration, because they believe that it affords them the right to point the finger somewhere else. You have probably met people who are suffering from this kind of frustration. They are the ones who cut you off on the highway and exhibit road rage. They are the ones who huff and puff when the checkout lines at the grocery store are too long and the cashiers are not fast enough for them. They are the ones who let their level of professional frustration spill over into their entire lives. The truth is that most of these people may have been, and may still be, courteous and positive. Their career situations have gotten so out of hand, however, that they feel helpless, and being rude seems their only release valve for their frustration.

By now, you know that these people can choose differently. They can start to explore options that will help them feel more in control of their lives. Many of them don't take that positive step because fear won't allow it. It requires a level of self-awareness and personal responsibility for someone to admit they have the power to change their circumstances.

Which type of frustration are you feeling? Whether your frustration is the healthy or unhealthy kind, you can learn to *turn your frustration into fascination.*

Here's how: If you are frustrated, chances are, you are stuck in a fixed mindset that says: *This is the status quo. No possibilities or opportunities exist here.* If you become curious, you turn your frustration into fascination. You can flip from a fixed mindset to a growth mindset where imagination, opportunities, and possibilities thrive. In this state of mind, you can start to explore the options you have to reach the desired F-Word: Financial Freedom.

"If you don't like something, change it.
If you can't change it, change your attitude."
—Maya Angelou

FEAR

What do you worry about?
What makes you afraid?
What causes anxiety for you?
What keeps you away from making a change?
What makes you run the other way when someone brings up the word change?
Are you even aware of all the voices of fear and all its disguises?
Let's find out.

For almost four decades, we have worked with people going through career transitions. We have assisted them as they fulfill their dreams and become self-sufficient. And, as we've accompanied them on the way to their goals, we have met many of their fears.

Most people in career transition worry about everything from whether they will be employable once they reach a certain age to the transferability of their skills at a time when traditional career options are becoming increasingly limited.

Others worry about the change they are about to go through while being terrified of the big unknown about something like self-employment. Many of these fears are fueled by false evidence that seems to be true. The acronym we often use for this mental state is F.E.A.R. (False Evidence Appearing Real).

Once we get outside our comfort zone, our anxiety levels and insecurities start to rise. This is normal. It happens to almost everyone. When it does, we start looking for reasons that something *won't* work. We manufacture scenarios and label them as evidence to talk ourselves out of taking the necessary steps toward change. We create our own False Evidence and make it Appear Real.

Any time you learn how to do something new or different, it will feel uncomfortable at first. When that discomfort and FEAR make you want to turn back, ask yourself these two questions:

1. Is it worth it to you to be temporarily uncomfortable if the potential results will exceed your current results?
2. Are you looking to be 100 percent comfortable, or are you looking to be successful in achieving your desired Income, Lifestyle, Wealth, and Equity?

Bear in mind that a little fear is normal when you contemplate something new, but it doesn't have to paralyze you. Be open to exploring the options you discover and let the facts speak for themselves. Don't let the fear of the unknown rob you of the opportunity to examine what's possible. Let the coaching experience and Journey of Discovery discern what is false evidence and what is real.

FEAR OF CHANGE

For many people, *change is a source of fear*—the fear of added stress, the fear of discomfort, or the fear of the unknown. Change is an inevitable part of life. In fact, in today's digital economy, change is the driving force. This means that those who view it with fear tend to spend far too much energy trying *unsuccessfully* to avoid it.

Change seems frightening because it threatens the comfort that we have constructed for ourselves. Feeling at risk, we try to create situations that we think will make us whole again, conditions and thoughts that will bring us back to the sense of security we used to feel. Which is just as impossible as trying to avoid change.

The only way to deal with change is to feel the fear and go through it anyway. No doubt, it requires courage. But there are a few things that can lessen the fears that accompany change.

The first is having someone you trust to support you.

The second is to manage the fear by keeping your eye on the ultimate goal, such as your dream of financial independence for yourself and your family A coach can help you in terms of support and focus.

---

*"Courage is not the absence of fear,
but rather the assessment that something
else is more important than fear."*
—Franklin D. Roosevelt

FEAR OF THE UNKNOWN

The *fear of the unknown* can also leave people in a frozen state—afraid of entering and exploring the new ground because they don't know what to expect or if they can handle what's coming. Fearful, they hold on to the familiar, even when the familiar has reached a point of being unbearable. These people may know what they need to do, but they simply can't take action because they think the risk involved with their career transition is too big.

The idea of self-employment can be a terrifying thing for many people for many reasons. While looking at new opportunities, people can feel pressured to make a decision, either to stay in their old jobs with the hope that the steady paychecks will continue or to take a risk and strike out on their own.

The irony is that, in today's job market, figuring out a way to become self-sufficient is probably the less risky choice.

The fear of the unknown can prevent people from making any decision. Equating *decision-making* with *making a bad or the wrong decision* some people simply refuse to act.

Take, for example, the fears surrounding self-employment. Often those fears are connected to concern about making the wrong decision. The consequence of ending up worse off than before is steep. Adding to the fear are tales of business failures. Everyone has heard horror stories about the number of people who start their businesses, only to have them go under after three, five, or even ten years.

As a result, many people associate being self-employed with a much higher risk of failure. Individuals fear being self-employed because they cannot escape the sense of insecurity that arises from the lack of a perceived corporate safety net. They wonder if they can truly do this on their own where others have failed.

Another fear that prevents people from making decisions or making a move toward self-employment is the belief that success requires a background in or a passion for that new type of business. This unfounded belief prompts some individuals to spend countless hours searching for *the right* business that best fits their passion, interests, prior experience, and skills.

What many people don't realize is that everything they enjoy doing now didn't particularly interest them until after they had experienced it. For example, you may never have considered learning to golf until someone talked you into taking lessons. You may have dismissed the game and even called it silly until you tried it. But after taking lessons, you might discover that you love the game of golf. To get there, though, you would have to set aside your preconceived ideas and be willing to give it a try.

Leaving your comfort zone never feels natural. But if you keep an open mind and educate yourself, what you will learn may surprise you. What if you discovered that there is a way to find a more fulfilling career than anything the corporate world has been able to offer?

The only way to beat the fear of the unknown is to take the first step. If you're afraid of getting in trouble, remember that you're already in bigger trouble if you ignore your heart. Allow your goals and dreams to guide you to new possibilities. If you listen to the voice of your fears, you'll live an empty life. But if you listen to the voice of your heart, you'll live a remarkable life.

Once you start to explore the possibilities, you will learn what works and what doesn't work for you, and you will soon gain clarity about what you need to do to achieve your desired Income, Lifestyle, Wealth, and Equity.

FEAR OF SUCCESS

Believe it or not, the *fear of success* stops more people than the fear of failure. Sure, we tend to be more aware of our fear of failing—the pain involved with that is usually more tangible, and the images more vivid. In many ways, this is part of the unconscious mind's brilliant strategy to keep us from seeing the real fear—the fear that we can be a total success.

Success has all kinds of repercussions and these by-products are the real causes of our fears. It is not success, per se, that we are afraid of. Rather, we're terrified of what we believe it will mean. With success comes higher expectations, possible jealousy from others, and the most dreaded consequence of all: change.

Consider these questions:

- Who will you become when you achieve even more success?
- How will your life change?
- What about your family?
- How will your relationships be affected by your success?

When you reflect on these questions, sometimes failing or at the very least complacency, seems like a cakewalk in comparison. But is that really what you'd rather do? Would you rather settle for mediocrity than strive for excellence?

It's important to identify what you're truly afraid of so you can collect the evidence to dismantle your fears. Approaching your options with a sense of curiosity instead of dread will empower you, and with each new piece of information, you'll start dissolving your fears.

FINANCES

The next F-word is *finances*. Many people limit their possibilities because they believe they don't have the money or they don't have enough money. They think they cannot afford to invest in their future. And yet so many are willing to go into debt for higher education without contemplating the potential return on investment. According to the Department of Education analysis, the typical undergraduate student with loans graduates with nearly $25,000 in debt. The White House further states that the skyrocketing cumulative federal student loan debt is $1.6 trillion—and rising—for more than 45 million borrowers.[21] On the other end of the spectrum, an AARP study found that 42 percent of adults forty-five and older identify as "lifelong learners," and many more say they intend to engage in learning as they age. If those who indicate they would engage in lifelong learning in the future were to do so, the lifelong-learning market would equate to more than 92 million people spending an estimated $6.9 billion annually.[22]

What are you willing to invest in yourself? If you took on debt, would it be good debt or bad debt? Would it be worth the cost long term, bringing you a solid return on your investment?

At this point, we're not going to dive into all the different ways to fund your dreams. After all, we are merely scratching the surface of what your Income, Lifestyle, Wealth, and Equity goals, needs, and expectations may be. But if *finances* is an F-word that makes it difficult for you to dream, we hope you'll set that aside with the knowledge that there are many different vehicles you could use to pursue your goals. For now, we want to encourage you to keep dreaming. Regardless of your financial situation, you are not confined to a career in the traditional job market.

Before you rule out any choices or limit yourself, consider all the possibilities, including how to fund them. Compare and contrast each option and determine the pros and cons of each. Systematically evaluate the potential ROI from an Income, Lifestyle, Wealth, and Equity perspective.

You might discover, as many of our clients have, that it can be less risky to diversify reactive investments to more proactive investment vehicles.

You may be surprised to discover what funds are available to you. Opportunities exist for all types of people and their varied financial situations.

Get the facts. Don't dismiss your dream for the fear that you could never afford it. Remember what John Wooden said: "It is what you learn after you think you know it all that really counts."[23]

FAMILY AND FRIENDS

The last of the F-words are *family and friends*. They are perhaps the most important influences on whether people decide to take the leap of faith, transition into self-sufficiency, and leave behind a traditional career. This is especially true for those whose family depends upon their income to survive.

It's, of course, important to consider the opinions and feelings of those you love when deciding on your future career path. After all, they will be affected by your choices. However, family and friends can become a significant roadblock to seizing your destiny and taking ownership of your career, and control of your Income, Lifestyle, Wealth, and Equity.

Your family may have relied on you, and possibly only you, to provide the security and stability they need to live and be happy. When something happens to undermine your ability to provide, such as a job change, you may feel a sense of shame and doubt. At the same time, your loved ones may feel alarmed, knowing you may no longer have the ability to provide for them at the same level you have in the past. This fear is the elephant in the room. No one talks about it, but everyone knows it's there, and its presence can exacerbate your fears about attempting to transfer into a more proactive and self-sufficient career.

Your family and friends aren't deliberately trying to pull you down. They just don't want you to fail—for your sake and theirs. Even if you know that you want to make a change because what you've been doing is no longer working for you (or perhaps never really did), chances are good that your friends and family members are stuck in the old paradigm that the corporate/employee route is best. As a result, they might try to discourage you.

Your loved ones fear the obstacles in your path and, like crabs in a basket, may try to pull you back. But it's not always for the reasons you may think. If you have ever been crabbing, you know that after you put a layer or two of crabs in a basket, you no longer need a lid. Throw a little crab bait in the basket, and whenever one of the crabs tries to climb out, the rest of the crabs reach up and pull it back down. Although it may look like they are trying to keep the potential escapee in the basket, what is really happening is that they are hanging on in hopes that they'll be able to get out with their compatriot. The crabs have the desire to escape, but they are too caught up in the old methods to see that what they are doing is more harmful than helpful.

In much the same way, your family and friends may be holding you back because they are fearful of being left behind. We all want to be part of something—a family, a group of friends, a team of coworkers—and it can be those very people who may make it even harder for you to make a change, especially if you are dealing with your doubts and fears. They want to protect you from what seems to be a certain catastrophe, so they direct a large dose of pessimism your way. If you're not careful, this can create a negative multiplier effect, which in turn generates more F.E.A.R. You may resort to inaction to appease family and friends—and avoid facing your own fear.

Involving your family early in your Journey of Discovery can help put at least some of their fears to rest. Although you can't control them, your courage may inspire them on their own journey. You might be the catalyst to help them evolve and grow or, at the very least, you may gain their support for the change you are seeking.

Just because people can't understand where you are going, it doesn't mean the destination does not exist. Some important questions to ask yourself are:

How would it make you feel if you had a clear vision of what you want to do, where you want to go, who you want to be, and what you could become and decided not to act on it? Could you live with yourself? Would you have any remorse?

IT IS ALL IN THE TIMING

No matter what fears people may or may not have about venturing into the sometimes-daunting world of self-sufficiency, some of them will always find a way of putting off taking that final leap. More often than not, once they've addressed all of the potential fears, choosing a path becomes an issue of timing.

In nearly four decades of empowering people, regardless of how good or bad the economy and job market have been, we have found that some people have always used one or the other as an excuse to say, "This isn't the right time to leave the conventional career path."

If things have been going well with the market and new businesses are flourishing, they don't want to risk the increased competition. If the economy has been on a downslide, they do not think starting a business is financially viable. After all, why risk starting something that will probably be wiped out by a recession?

No matter what, there is always a reason to avoid making a move. They want a 100 percent guarantee in a world where nothing is guaranteed. They try to disprove every opportunity to keep from facing the hardest fact of all: the only things keeping them from the success of that opportunity are their own fears, most of which are unfounded.

Sometimes we need to be okay with the fact that all we can do is make the best possible choice. We are not talking about being reckless but about making an informed choice. And getting to work on making whatever we've committed to doing a reality so that, over time, it can become the best decision we've ever made.

MOVING INTO THE FUTURE

Some people see the gap between their current situation and the success they imagine and wonder whether they can survive the leap. They're so busy focusing on what they could lose that they can't see what they might gain.

While some people remain stuck, an ever-increasing number of people are taking the leap. They are moving from unemployment, *under*employment, or even gainful but unfulfilling employment to a place of empowerment. And many have discovered that having a Career Ownership Coach helps pave the way for a smoother launch and landing.

A coach can provide a mental safety net so you can make the jump from where you are to where you want to be. A coach can't jump for you. You still have to leap, but you don't have to do it alone.

Transformation begins when you look beyond your current situation to see what *could* be. Once you create a vision for your life, use that as your north star to guide you as you explore the possibilities that have the potential to help you reach your goals, needs, and expectations. Many different types of vehicles exist that can be used to help transport you to the life you desire. Your role is to embark on the Journey of Discovery and learn about these options.

In the next chapter, we'll explore the different vehicles that can get you to your dream life so that you can determine which one is right for you.

CHAPTER 4

MAKE THE BEST CHOICE FOR YOU

Your dream requires a unique vehicle.

Dreams don't work unless you do.
—John Maxwell

e started this Journey of Discovery by reviewing the circumstances that brought you to this point of inquiry and pursuit of something better. Then you looked inward and answered some critical questions designed to help you create and clarify the new version of yourself–your YOU 2.0©.

In the previous chapter, we examined the most common inner struggles people face when considering the possibilities for the future. Hopefully, you saw that you are not alone if you are dealing with any doubts, fears, or the influence of those you love. Those barriers are common and felt by almost everyone who is considering change, regardless of what type of change it is.

Now it's time to look outward again but with a different perspective—one of being empowered to change your circumstances by taking personal responsibility and making different choices. But instead of having a mindset of, "This will never work!" what if you embraced a mindset of "What would it take to make this work?"

Most people have to engage in some kind of activity to generate the income they need to live. Some people might have more than enough money, but the time they must invest to generate that income comes at a serious cost—both personally and professionally. In this chapter, we'll examine the various vehicles you can use to explore those that will allow you to move past trading time for money.

The most common options available to us include the job market, the stock market, real estate investments, entrepreneurship, and owning a business of some kind. Let's explore the pros and cons of each of these in a little more detail.

THE JOB MARKET

The education system in the United States prepares children for the job market. More specifically (and detrimentally) the education system still tends to prepare people to be industrial workers—cogs in a system rather than the thinkers who create new and better systems. This is changing, but the change is coming at a much slower rate than the advancement of technology. Perhaps this is why traditional jobs are one of the most commonly employed vehicles. When you were growing up, you probably had at least one teacher or parent advise you to work hard and get good grades so that you could get a good job.

For many people, a job in the corporate world is (or was) the dream job. We say *was* because, as we discussed early on in this book, discontent with the corporate world is common today. Job security is a dream from a bygone era. More and more corporate jobs disappear every day due to economic fluctuations, cheaper labor in foreign countries, new technology, younger workers, and so on. Employees all too often feel cheated by the trade-offs they have to make working in the corporate world.

Those who remain in the job market may do so for a few different reasons. Some, as we discussed in the previous chapter, may fear making the leap to something different. Others, however, are truly content to be employees. They enjoy the relational structure of the workplace. For many, it is a great opportunity to learn and be exposed to things that they otherwise would not be. Many are comfortable with a little less control over their workload and schedule if it means they don't have to be responsible for payroll, manage people, make major decisions, and can go home at the end of the day and leave their jobs behind. They prefer routine over responsibility and feel a sense of security working for someone else.

The world needs people who are ready, willing, and able to be employees. Our economic structure depends on people filling these roles. And even though the job market is not what it used to be, there are still some good jobs out there. Some companies do care for, challenge, and fairly compensate their employees.

Some of our clients, in fact, have found great success in the job market with companies just like that. They've enjoyed their corporate careers and came to The Entrepreneur's Source for coaching, not because they were dissatisfied with their career in the job market, but because they were simply at a point where they want to add to their portfolio and diversify their earnings options.

If that sounds like you, congratulations. Your experience is the exception rather than the rule, and it simply means you are at a point where you'd like to use multiple vehicles to reach your Income, Lifestyle, Wealth, and Equity goals.

Depending on who you are and what you value, you may be one of those people who just never were meant to be an employee. Perhaps you value freedom and indepen- dence more than the rigid structure of a traditional job. Perhaps you like control and having equity in something. If that's true, then being an employee may not be the right fit for you. That means, if you are currently an employee, you are likely experiencing some dissatisfaction. You may be feeling like you don't fit, or something is missing, or that you are working against your grain. Some of the other vehicles we are about to explore may be more appealing to you.

THE STOCK MARKET, REAL ESTATE, AND OTHER INVESTMENTS

Investing is another vehicle for reaching your I.L.W.E. goals, and for many people, this is the right strategy. Although professional investing is not for everyone, investors and investment opportunities span the gamut. There are proactive investors and passive investors, short-term and long-term investors. Some people invest in ideas, other people, startups, art, collectibles, markets, real estate, cryptocurrencies, and a plethora of other things.

With the variety of investment options available, the important question to ask yourself is this: *Do I have a proper strategy and the mindset it takes to be a successful investor?* Stock, bond, crypto, and real estate markets fluctuate with the economy and require not only interest, knowledge, and aptitude in these fields but also a high tolerance for risk, especially if you don't know what you are doing. Many people shy away from investing due to their lack of knowledge and education and the lack of control inherent to many of these opportunities.

For the majority of people, investing is a way to diversify income and build wealth, but they don't consider it a full-time occupation because the perception of risk feels too great to be reliable. Because of this, most investors are passive and reactive, meaning they have relinquished control to someone else or the market. Ironically, the reason investing feels risky to these same people is because their passive or reactive approach makes them subject to the whims of the economy, the markets, or their financial advisors. Having invested their money, they are hoping for a return. But as James Cameron said, "Hope is not a strategy."

ENTREPRENEURSHIP AND BUSINESS OWNERSHIP

Entrepreneurship, like investing, is more like a fleet of vehicles than a single opportunity. Before we explore the different vehicles, let's look at some of the reasons you might be considering this particular option. Consider the following questions:

- Do you identify with being an entrepreneur? Do you have an entrepreneurial itch?
- If you desire to be an entrepreneur, what is driving that motivation?
- Are you so disenchanted with your job that striking out on your own feels like it is the right thing to do?
- Have you always had the desire to be your own boss?
- Or do you have an idea that is haunting you and keeping you up at night—a product or service that you wish to bring to the marketplace?

We ask you these questions because it's important to know your motivation. The truth is that sometimes people leap into entrepreneurship with the wrong mindset or unrealistic expectations.

According to Michael Gerber, author of E-Myth, "The excitement of independence associated with getting rid of the boss is almost always fueled by a flawed understanding of what being on your own means. Most small businesses are started by technicians rather than by true entrepreneurs."[24]

The technician believes in the fatal assumption that because he or she knows how to do the work—whether graphic design, engineering, cooking a great dinner, repairing an automobile, snowboarding, or otherwise—they can turn that capability into a business that frees them from the boss. The graphic designer creates a graphic design business. The technologist creates a technology-based business. The cook creates a restaurant. The mechanic creates an auto repair business. The snowboarder creates a snowboarding business.

But instead of freeing themselves from the boss, they have become their own boss, and they're now—with absolutely no understanding about how it happened—working for a lunatic and doing what they know how to do but in greater volume than before.[25]

Some people leap without understanding the scope of the decision. Others, who may desire to leave the job market, may refuse to make the leap because they do not see themselves as entrepreneurial. They don't feel bold enough or creative enough. Even if they have a rough idea for a business, the risks of failure seem too high. Because they do not identify with being an entrepreneur, they think they just need to deal with the devil they know (the job market), rather than the one they don't (business ownership).

Granted, as with all vehicles, business ownership has inherent risks. But just as not all jobs are bad. nor are all investments exceptionally risky, not all business formats are created equally. And you don't necessarily need to identify with being an entrepreneur to be a successful business owner.

Let's explore some of the different business ownership formats in more detail.

INDEPENDENT BUSINESS OWNERSHIP

Starting an independent business from scratch comes at a cost. Business ownership requires knowledge, systems, resources, and expertise. Before you even open your doors for business, you can incur significant costs and need to gain the required knowledge associated with market research, equipment, store design and layout, pricing, public relations, testing the model, putting an infrastructure in place, developing technology, and hiring and training employees.

An independent business owner has to know or learn about many aspects of starting and operating a business—things that have nothing to do with the services or products it offers. Independent business owners have to know about marketing, finance, accounting, operations, customer service, equipment, vendor relations, price negotiations, pricing, employee management, and customer retention, among many other disciplines.

They also have to keep ahead of the competition and invest money and resources in research and development to stay ahead of the game. They must create a demand for their products and services by building a strong brand. If they want to succeed but don't have all of this knowledge and experience, they have to get it somewhere else. They will have to hire employees or experts in these areas, which can be very expensive.

Independent business owners have to develop and prove their business model. They don't have a successful example to follow. They may be able to get some information about similar businesses, but they have to create their own *secret sauce*. If they don't do well, most small independent business owners blame the economy or the competition from the large chains. Sometimes, however, their failure to achieve the results they want and need is the result of something they are missing, but they're too close to the problem to see it. Unless they hire an outside consultant or business coach, they may never know what is causing their problem.

One of the most disturbing characteristics of owning an independent business is the fact that you are all alone. There is no support mechanism behind you, no one to call when you have a question or a problem, and no one who can listen to your woes and help you get out of your own way to achieve the results you desire. There is no one to provide training when there is a gap in knowledge or experience, no one to even recognize when there is a gap. It's just you. This aloneness can feel especially distressing if you are accustomed to working for someone else or within a team environment.

There are some lone rangers out there for whom not having a support team is not a problem. These people prefer to be alone and to have full responsibility for everything. They are risk-takers and love to wear many hats, at least in the beginning. They thrive on the pursuit of opportunity. They are true entrepreneurs.

Perhaps you fit this mold. If you do, you're in the minority. (In fact, less than 10 percent of the population is well suited for this path.) You are a maverick and visionary, and we applaud you.

Every great business on earth today started as someone's crazy idea. The reason we applaud the true entrepreneur is that your vision is strong enough to combat those naysayers who enthusiastically tell you that your idea is insane and that it will never work and that you are wasting your time.

When Terry started The Entrepreneur's Source, countless people told him that his idea wouldn't work. A former business partner told him, "You are wasting your time with those tire kickers and dreamers."

But instead of being discouraged, this comment had the opposite effect. That word dreamer fueled a fire in Terry because he saw himself as a dreamer. His vision was to help others make their dreams a reality so they could create a better and brighter future. Walt Disney's quote gave him all the inspiration he needed: "All your dreams can come true if you have the courage to pursue them."

Despite the odds and the challenges, a true entrepreneur will prove the rest of the world wrong. Everyone else benefits from their innovation.

FRANCHISE OWNERSHIP

For many, being independent and creating a business from scratch holds little appeal. Most people prefer a proven roadmap to follow and a team to support them in their own business. The good news is that there are opportunities to own and operate a business that don't require the owner to be solely responsible for every facet of the business.

Franchising is an option that allows you to be in business for yourself, but not by yourself. If the first thing that comes to mind when you hear the word franchise is fast food and French fries, hang on. Franchising is so much more than that.

The great majority of franchise companies started as independent businesses that reached a certain level of success. Those independent small businesses that we spoke about before, then decided to scale it up by sharing their winning formula with people who are willing to follow their proven system. Franchisors (the companies that franchise their businesses) share their experience with franchisees (those people who invest in the opportunity). They provide them with comprehensive training, support programs, and the roadmap needed to replicate business results.

Most franchising opportunities require no experience or industry background. Most franchise companies prefer people who have no prior experience in their type of business to join as franchisees. Why is that? Because franchising is all about replicating a business's success through a proven SYSTEM—a model that affords you to Save Yourself Significant Time, Energy, and Money.

Franchising is one of the few commercial interactions based on creating and sustaining an interdependent win-win relationship. The success of a franchise company depends on the success of its franchisees and vice versa. This interdependence tends to create a healthy environment where members support rather than compete with each other, and where they motivate, celebrate, and are ready to assist other franchisees.

Although the premises of franchising apply to all franchise companies, as with every other vehicle, not all franchise opportunities or companies are created equally, nor are they right for everyone. The potential for win-win relationships, support, a successful formula, and winning tools exists in every company, but each concept is different. Likewise, how these elements manifest in the company depends on many factors.

THE SEVEN MYTHS OF FRANCHISE OWNERSHIP

Make sure these myths are not holding you back from, at the very least, taking a look at franchising.

Myth 1: Finding the right business will make me successful.

Truth: there isn't a *right* business or a *wrong* business. What may be right for one person may not be right for the next. So even though each franchise system gives its franchisees a proven system to follow, it is up to the individual—you—to execute it and make it work.

When you look at the most successful franchise concepts today, there will be some owners who do extremely well and some who don't. Why is that? Well, one way to find out is to discover what the successful owners did that the others didn't. Then do some self-reflection and determine whether you are willing to do what it takes to be one of the successful owners. The great thing about franchise concepts is that you have multiple existing businesses that you can study and learn from, compared to an independent business, where only one exists or a business that has been ideated but still lacks proof of concept.

Keep this in mind: The business does not make you successful. *You* make the business successful. Don't sell yourself short. You're already successful in key areas of your career and your life. A coach can help you think about how some of those skills and attributes are transferable.

Myth 2: The secret to success is to find a career doing something I love.

Truth: Businesses founded on the owner's background, experience, or knowledge have the highest incidence of failure. *Ouch.* That seems counterintuitive, doesn't it? The reality is that business owners have various responsibilities ranging from business development to accounting to delivering the service or product and more. If you create a business around a hobby or a passion and ignore the other important business elements, the thing you used to love so much will soon become the thing you dread. On the flip side, if you restrict your options to things that you're already good at or already love, you shut down a universe of possibilities.

Here's a fun fact: Most franchise business owners are in a business today that they had no previous experience in or are in an industry they had no initial affinity toward. Crazy, right? And yet, franchise owners commonly outperform their independent counterparts. How do we know this? In our almost forty years of working with clients to explore alternate career options, 95 percent of those who have chosen a franchise have ended up in one they admit they never would have looked at on their own—or had looked at but dismissed prematurely.

Myth 3: I'll know the right opportunity when I see it.

Truth: Believing that you'll fall in love at first sight is a trap. Many people make an emotional connection with a career and invest months of hard work only to find that it doesn't meet their goals, needs, and expectations. A better path to follow is to be curious and seek the truth. Don't make an impulsive or emotional decision. Gather the facts. Just as we advise clients to avoid prematurely dismissing options, we ask them to gather the facts and table their emotions, even if they are really excited about a particular opportunity.

Wouldn't it be fascinating to find out why others invested in a franchise? Wouldn't it be interesting to find out whether they always wanted to be in a business like this or what their motivations were? Are they getting the ROI they were hoping for? Are they happy and would they do it again? A coach helps you avoid the pitfalls of your limiting beliefs and of leaping without looking at the big picture—and the details.

**Myth 4: I can't be in the _____ business.
I don't know a *blankety-blank* thing about _____!**

Truth: The good news is you don't have to know anything about whatever it is you put in that blank. You hire people who do. Rather than working in the business, your role is to work on the business. What if you thought of your role as being in the business of growing a business? Remember that in a franchise system, a good franchisor provides systems, tools, and operating methods so you don't need to figure out everything by yourself.

Myth 5: Corporate HQ will dictate everything.

Truth: The fear that you won't have any control in a franchise is unfounded. Franchisors provide the framework, but as the franchisee, you manage, market, and promote the business. You're in charge. Remember, franchising is based on interdependent, win-win relationships. Franchisors don't win unless you win. There has never been a successful franchisor without successful franchisees.

Myth 6: I can't be creative in a franchise.

Truth: Creativity comes in managing and marketing a proven process. And there's plenty of room for your ideas. You'd be astonished to know how many product and service innovations have come from franchisees, not the parent company.

Myth 7: A franchise requires more money than I can afford.

Truth: You may be surprised. Our most successful clients have seen acquiring the rights to operate a franchise as an investment—and they get a return on that investment. Before you let money concerns squelch your future, seek the facts. Engage with a coach. Most of our clients have been amazed at the array of industries franchise concepts are a part of and the many ways to fund them.

You don't know what you don't know. We have been able to help clients whose accountants were dumbfounded and amazed at options available to them that even they had never heard of.

Give Yourself Permission to Learn

Even if you conclude that you want to explore franchising as a possible vehicle to achieve the Income, Lifestyle, Wealth, and Equity you desire, you still have a lot of work ahead of you to discern which opportunity suits you best.

Feel a little overwhelmed? We understand. After all, there are thousands of franchise opportunities to choose from. You may be wondering:

Where do I start? How many opportunities do I need to investigate? When do I know that I have found the right opportunity? How do I know I am making the right decision?

These are all logical questions to ask down the road, but remember: 1) right now, you are still on your Journey of Discovery, and 2) you don't have to go on this journey alone. Before you try to ask or answer a ton of questions, give yourself time to learn.

Maintain a Growth Mindset

If you find yourself intimidated by the variety of possibilities or can't see a way out of the job market because you don't identify with being an investor, a business owner, or an entrepreneur, it may be because mindsets or misconceptions are clouding your ability to dream. Remember, at this point, the focus is on education and exploration. You don't need to leap off any cliffs or make a reckless decision.

We encourage you to maintain an open mindset—one that allows you to expand your thinking about what's possible. Don't let misguided beliefs or myths, like the seven we've listed above, prevent you from experiencing the Income, Lifestyle, Wealth, and Equity you desire. Just be open to learning what it will take to do what you've never done before and have what you've never had before so that you can be who you want to be.

A Career Ownership Coach may be just the resource you need. As an organization, we have helped tens of thousands of people just like you make successful career transitions by exploring various vehicles, even those they had prematurely dismissed. When re-examining them from a different perspective, many realize that these may have the potential to meet or exceed their goals, needs, and expectations to achieve their desired Income, Lifestyle, Wealth, and Equity. Our passion is assisting curious people on their unique journey.

CHAPTER 5

NO ONE NEEDS
TO WALK ALONE

Being open to coaching makes all the difference.

*A coach is someone that sees beyond your limits and
guides you to greatness.*

—Michael Jordan

Steve Jobs had a coach. Oprah Winfrey has a coach. Tom Brady has a coach. So, why shouldn't you have one? The more successful people become, the more they realize that it's impossible to be an expert at everything. Whether it's a personal coach, a sports coach, a business coach, or a Career Ownership Coach, successful people enlist the assistance of others.

A Career Ownership Coach provides a safe environment. They ask thought-provoking and tough questions to challenge your thinking and mindset, and they hold up a mirror so you can become accountable to yourself and allow yourself to reach your maximum potential.

Coaches assist clients in three important ways:

1. **Education**—A coach provides a safe space for you to learn and educate yourself and to examine areas of your life that hold the answer to your future.
2. **Awareness**—A coach creates an environment for you to become aware of what is and what could be possible for you.
3. **Discovery**—A coach can help you discover what's possible and what you need to do to make your dreams a reality by holding you accountable to what you say you want as it relates to your goals, needs, and expectations.

Engaging with a Career Ownership Coach allows you to participate in a coaching experience that helps you see beyond your blind spots and challenges you to explore what lies outside your comfort zone. Let's face it, generally, we only allow ourselves to see things we understand or about which we have firsthand knowledge.

The optimal coaching experience is designed to help you look within to determine your path to achieving your career and lifestyle goals, including your longer-term wealth and equity goals. If you are not where you want to be, working with a coach—someone who will come alongside you—will help you explore what's possible. When you are truly open to coaching, you will become aware of options and opportunities you may have never considered previously.

Some of the possibilities you explore with your coach may seem intimidating at first. When you have no experience in an area and thus lack a frame of reference for an opportunity, it can seem overwhelming. Add in the noise of people's stories of fear or failure, and you may be tempted to run back to your dissatisfying but familiar comfort zone. This is where a Career Ownership Coach can help you put your emotions and biases on hold so you can give yourself time to gather the facts you need to find what you are seeking—to discover a better way to reach your goals.

Of course, the vast majority of people want to be self-sufficient. But that is not the same as wanting to be a business owner or going into business for yourself.

We estimate about 75 percent of the adult population want to be self-sufficient, but most of them are scared to death about business ownership. In our experience, only 5 percent are ready, willing, and able to do something about their desire. The others might be ready someday, but they could benefit from coaching first. They need someone who believes in their potential and future more than they do at the moment.

In the face of fear, it is natural for your mind to search for examples where something didn't work, where someone had regrets, or where businesses failed. Remember, just because something is scary, doesn't mean you shouldn't explore it and educate yourself. Knowledge is power and a weapon against fear.

Speaking of fear, don't expect this emotion to vanish entirely, even when you gain knowledge. Fear can steal your dreams, but only *if* you let it. You can learn to manage fear by recognizing that it is often simply false evidence appearing real. Using information, facts, and knowledge, you can determine what is true and what isn't. The power of working with a coach is that you learn to see through the fear so you can look at possibilities in a way you may never have been able to before. At the end of the day, wouldn't you rather make informed choices based on facts rather than emotions?

THE PILLARS OF A QUALITY COACHING EXPERIENCE

There is a growing distrust in organizations and institutions including governments, media, and corporations. The world where we have replaced a handshake and verbal agreements, which meant everything, with mistrust and skepticism. Our world craves trustworthy leaders who have our best interests in mind. For this reason, leadership, relationship, and opportunity are the three pillars of our coaching experience.

LEADERSHIP

Leaders help people overcome fear and navigate confusion. Good coaches serve a similar role.

Our clients know that they may never reach those distant goals on their horizon if they travel alone—or if they do, it will take them much longer than necessary. They know that having a guide who can lead the way and provide direction as well as a safe space to grow and learn will help them achieve their goals faster.

As an organization, we have made it our mission to hone our craft and our tools to empower people looking to explore their possibilities, options, and dreams. Our coaches find great joy in leading clients like you through peaks of excitement for the future and valleys of doubt and fear. We provide the structure you need to help you locate and leverage your internal compass. When fear and doubt raise their ugly heads, we help you rescue your dream and bring you back to what's important to you.

RELATIONSHIP

The search for leadership begins by asking, "Who can give me direction?" But there's more to coaching than direction. The relationship factor asks the equally important question, "Who can I trust?" Failed pension plans, dead-end jobs irrelevant higher education, and other factors have caused many people to doubt people, systems, and institutions that promised so much.

NO ONE NEEDS TO WALK ALONE

Trust is earned. We understand that—which is why our pledge to those who want to learn and explore is that it is all about *you*: your goals, your needs, and your expectations. Our only request is that you keep an open mind and make no decisions prematurely. This relationship can open a new world of possibilities.

OPPORTUNITY

Once leadership and relationships have been established, people find the confidence to explore possibilities they may never have considered before. With the help of someone they trust, they can see the potential in themselves and in the ideas that they may have previously dismissed. The result of this openness to education and exploration is opportunity.

Working with a trusted coach who acts as a sounding board and provides direction makes it easier for you to explore options in a safe space. When the pressure is off, there's no agenda. Everyone benefits. We are merely embarking on a Journey of Discovery, seeing past fears and frustrations. This new focus opens opportunities for what lies ahead. In this environment, mindsets are transformed.

In the past forty years, tens of thousands of people have been empowered by our coaches and our systems. The benefits of exploring new information about non-conventional career choices are tremendous, even if you do not act on that knowledge immediately.

FROM SEEKING TO UNDERSTANDING

So, what does it look like to work with a Career Ownership Coach? We've covered some of what you can expect already. We start the journey by inviting you to take time to think introspectively about where you are in your life and where you want to be. Together, you and your coach will create mutual trust and freedom to explore your life today and tomorrow without any fear or risk.

Although key elements, such as leadership, relationships, and opportunities, may have been missing from your life, you can start experiencing them right now. Within this structure, you can begin to clarify your objectives—dream your dreams— while knowing you have people to support and guide you along the way.

Here are some questions to get you started:

- Where are you in your career?
- How can you change your current situation?
- What motivates you?
- What would you do if you knew you could not fail?
- How would your family feel if you decided to try a new career path?
- If we looked at your life a year from today, what has to have happened during that period, both personally and professionally, for you to be happy with your progress?

Your journey with your coach is about helping you clarify all these things and more. Many times, your coach will ask you questions and draw you into candid conversations about how you see your future. You may find yourself expressing thoughts and ideas that you haven't shared or discussed with your closest friends or spouse yet. Maybe you've never even had these conversations with yourself. The Journey of Discovery is about exploring your possibilities, options, and dreams. As you connect on a human level, you'll question, listen, and explore your ideas more deeply.

Even knowing what to expect from the coaching experience, you may still feel nervous. The unknown can be exhilarating and scary. Change by definition is uncomfortable.

It's a perfectly normal feeling. Whether you're considering stepping out of the traditional career mold, switching career paths, or investing in yourself, embarking on a new path can be a frightening prospect. One coaching session is not enough to eliminate all of those fears. It would not be abnormal if you didn't feel some anxiety about leaving your comfort zone. However, the information you discover will certainly help ease the fears you feel over time.

Remember, fear and discomfort are only temporary. If you could see the glorious other side, then taking this first step would feel much easier.

One of the benefits of our coaching experience is that it allows people to reframe any situation. For instance, it can be demoralizing to feel as if you are trapped on the career hamster wheel with no prospect of ever being able to create long-lasting wealth or a legacy. But what if you were to find out that does not need to be the case? Would that realization make a difference in your mindset and ignite the spark you need to dream again? Of course, it would! And that new mindset is what you need to turn your dreams into reality.

Or how about reframing a situation that, at the present moment, seems like the most terrible thing that has ever happened? The prospect of losing your job or the actual experience of losing it can be devastating. But what if a trusted coach could help you see that it may not be as bad as you think—that what seems like a hopeless situation is truly the beginning of a better and brighter future? What if the saying: "You have to lose something to gain something" applies to your job and career too?

What if this dire situation you're in was the start of a new, rich and fulfilling life?

Sometimes you need someone outside yourself and your circle to help you see beyond your circumstances. A coach can be the perfect person to fill that role.

CRITICAL INGREDIENTS FOR A SUCCESSFUL JOURNEY OF DISCOVERY

Are you intrigued by the idea of being your own boss or the possibility of being in business for yourself, but not by yourself? What if you could learn about different business models from the inside out, rather than from a website? That, too, is part of the Journey of Discovery. But don't expect to fall in love at first sight. Remember one of the myths we covered in a previous chapter, about how most of us often think finding the right opportunity will be like love at first sight? It's not. You might not even like some of the opportunities you learn about, at least not at first. That's okay. As you learn about different business models, fight the urge to think you have to choose the *right* one. Remember, for most, the business is not the dream, but the vehicle to the dream.

Your journey isn't about making decisions. Rather, it's about learning. Exploring all the options through a lens of what is possible, learning about what they have to offer, and talking to people who are leveraging different opportunities as the vehicle to their dreams will further clarify what you desire in life.

Your job is to remain open and have a beginner's mind. Zen Master Suzuki said: "In the beginner's mind there are many possibilities."[26]

Your call to adventure requires only two important things for it to unlock the door to new possibilities:

1. Keep an open mind.
2. Make no decisions.

This will allow you to have a successful Journey of Discovery to help you reach your goals and your YOU 2.0®. You can go from an employee mindset (or even unemployment) to *empowerment*.

Our objective is to help you become more aware of opportunities you might never have considered before. Things that you may have previously dismissed without proper examination can hold the key to your future success in achieving the Income, Lifestyle, Wealth, and Equity you desire. The key isn't to look for evidence to prove your preconceptions right. Instead, it's to exploring, learning, and being fascinated by the discovery of new information and options that you had never thought possible.

Are you committed enough to your dreams to keep an open mind? If you aren't, there is little value anyone can provide to you.

Although a Career Ownership Coach can act as a guide throughout this journey, you are still in charge of your learning and in charge of how fast or slow you want to go. A coach can support you and challenge you. A coach will highlight what may be limiting beliefs. A coach will help you look beyond your blind spots as you work on defining your dreams and learning about the possible vehicles to help you attain your goals, needs, and expectations. A coach will provide you with education and tools that help you get outside your comfort zone. For coaching to work, however, you must commit to keeping an open mind by not making premature decisions.

Expect that there are times when your coach will challenge you and hold you accountable for what you say you want. We often call that having "carefrontations" with our clients. We know that following your dream, changing direction, and pursuing a new career path can feel like navigating uncharted waters. It's tough sometimes, but we are here for you. We believe everybody has a dream worth pursuing.

Remember, this is a time for exploration. Many people are too afraid of change to take this initial step. But you are different. You have seized the opportunity to explore the world of self-sufficiency and financial independence. Now you must stay on the path that can take you there.

We believe in your possibilities, your options, and your dreams. Do you?

OUR UNIQUE COACHING METHODOLOGY

Throughout this book, we have talked a great deal about bridging the gap between your current situation and a brighter future full of greater Income, Lifestyle, Wealth, and Equity. We have explored what it means to move from unemployment, underemployment, or even employment to empowerment.

Maybe you're already familiar with the power of coaching. Maybe you're already working with an Entrepreneur's Source Career Ownership Coach, and you have developed an appreciation for why they do what they do. Or maybe you're at the point where you are ready to engage a coach.

Our commitment is to support anyone who has a dream and needs help to make it a reality. We know you will benefit from the value our coaching relationship brings. Let's take a look at what makes the relationship between The Entrepreneur's Source coaches and our clients so unique.

BELIEVING IN THE DREAM

A central characteristic of our coaches is that they often believe in your dream more than you do. You might wonder how that is even possible.

Let's go back to the weight loss analogy we used earlier in the book. We said everybody knows what it takes to lose weight. By and large, it involves eating less and exercising more. What prevents most people from accomplishing their weight loss goals is the lack of correct habits, discipline, or willpower to endure and keep the commitment in times of temptation or stress.

Giving up on the desired result in the short term is almost always easier than developing the habits that will ultimately give you what you say you want. The dream to be self-sufficient is no different in that it can feel easier to stick with the safe and familiar career path, even if you know what you need to do to create the changes you want. But there is one big difference in that you may not know or be able to see what you need to change—at least not without the help of a coach. Sometimes your dreams are on the other side of blinders you may not even be aware you're wearing.

Being blind to those possibilities doesn't mean there is anything wrong with you. It simply means that no one has given you the information you need. Or perhaps you haven't given yourself permission to learn and explore or dared to look beyond what you already know to find a new or better path. This is where our coaches come into the picture and serve as your dream champion.

Your coach's role is to guide you into the land of possibilities and help you establish the right relationships by providing the leadership that will allow you to look at things from a different perspective. Your coach wants you to see the opportunities that exist beyond your current comfort zone.

One of the key factors in our methodology is that it isn't about selling you features or benefits. It is not about selling you anything. Our coaches are there solely to guide you to a place of clarity that you would normally not be able to reach on your own. It is about creating an environment and establishing that sense of leadership and relationship that will allow this discovery to happen.

We help you look inward to gain clarity about what you want more of and less of in life, which empowers you to reconnect with your primary aim. In addition, our coaching experience offers practical examples of business models for you to learn about. It is at the point of exploring possibilities that most people forget about the commitment to having an open mind and not making decisions. Preconceptions and fear take over. Many people are tempted to fall into this trap and forget about the main goal of learning and discovery, *not* deciding.

When presented with business models, many of our clients' first reactions include statements such as:

- "I don't like any of these."
- "They have nothing to do with my experience or personality."
- "I just don't like them."
- "There is no way that I will ever do that or want to be a part of that."

That's often the voice of fear talking. The business models are unfamiliar and even considering them is an exercise outside of most people's comfort zones. The new and unknown can seem scary.

Sometimes it isn't fear but outdated mindsets. People assume that choosing a new career path should feel like falling in love. The common misconception is that even if they don't know exactly what they are looking for, they will know it when they see it.

As Career Ownership Coaches, we know it is our job to challenge limiting beliefs and shine a light on their blind spots. We want to make sure that false evidence appearing real doesn't hold them back from their greatness.

If you are worried that the same may happen to you and that your fears will keep you away from your goals, don't fret. We've been here many times with other clients.

We will simply remind you of your vision for your future. We will make you aware of your blind spots and we will bring you back to what's important to you.

Our goal is to help you reach clarity about what it will take to make *your* dreams come true. Once you have clarity, you will see the abundance of possibilities right in front of you. Your worldview may forever change. What an exciting thought, indeed!

PART 3

RECLAIM

CHAPTER 6

THERE'S NO TIME LIKE
THE PRESENT

**When you prepare for the moment,
the moment is prepared for you.**

*Time is your most precious resource;
make every minute count.*

—Brian Tracy

L et's recap all the progress you've already made. You experienced some of what The Entrepreneur's Source Journey of Discovery is about. You've thought and explored what the next version of you, YOU 2.0, could be. You've defined your goals, needs, and expectations around Income, Lifestyle, Wealth, and Equity. You've challenged some of your perceptions about the job market, investments, entrepreneurship, business ownership, and what it takes to be self-sufficient. You've weighed the pros and cons of the different vehicles to get you to your dream of financial independence. Or have you really? Just because you've read a few chapters in a book, does that mean that you have invested the time and energy to dig deep and do some soul-searching? Just because you read about coaching does it mean that you've had the opportunity to experience the benefits of what a good coaching session can do for you?

This is only the beginning of the journey, but we know that as we've piqued your curiosity about what's possible, you've already begun to make progress toward your new future, and for that, we want to congratulate you.

You've come a long way. Now you might be wondering where to go from here.

In this chapter, we'll take a closer look at two of the perceived obstacles that can trip you up: funding and indecision.

FINANCING THE FUTURE

How do you fund your transition from walking away from a traditional job and a steady paycheck while maintaining the financial necessities and responsibilities of running a household? For many people, this question can be one of the most difficult.

Perhaps your kids take piano lessons or need money for college tuition. Maybe your needs are even more basic, like groceries. Either way, if you are like most households, you have a monthly budget that needs to be met. That means intentionally leaving a steady paycheck, even with the prospect of self-sufficiency on the horizon, can be a financially frightening idea.

The key here is to budget properly. If you were beginning a new job, in all likelihood, you would begin with a salary that would increase the longer you remained in your position or the more competently you handled the job. The transition phase from employee to self-employed works in the same way. Essentially, you will be cutting yourself a paycheck and you have to plan that, at first, it will be a smaller paycheck than in the future.

At the beginning of your planning phase, sit down and draw up a monthly budget, figuring out exactly how much you and your family will need to maintain your lifestyle with all of its necessities and activities. Then consider what you could possibly cut out or live without for a short period. How long could you live without those things?

Obviously, you don't want to go backward and give up the things you need or love. But sometimes a temporary sacrifice can help you reach your ultimate goals. By finding a balance in your finances and budgeting the correct amount of money, you can determine whether you have enough to see your family through the transition phase.

Ultimately, you will be investing in yourself and them. We've already discussed the emotions and fears you and your loved ones might be feeling as you face a career transition. That awareness puts you in a position to handle those emotions well. From your well-informed vantage point, you can shift the questions regarding funding your investment in yourself and your future from wondering *whether* you can make it happen from a financial standpoint to *how* to make it happen.

One important thing to learn during this phase of exploration is how to turn reactive investments into proactive investment vehicles. This starts with understanding the difference between investing money and spending money.

When you spend money on something, you are likely not thinking about it as an asset that will generate cash flow or provide a return on investment (ROI). By definition, the expectation of an investment is that it should give you a return on the money you put into it. If you do not have reasonable confidence that your investment will provide a return, why invest?

Reactive investments, like having an advisor or a firm invest on your behalf in the stock market, as is commonly done with retirement plans, offer little control. This lack of control can be incredibly frustrating and is what drives some people to diversify and invest in opportunities over which they have more control. These proactive investments, such as becoming a business owner, allow their owners to better predict, or at least have more control over, their potential ROI.

You may think it's all well and good to tighten the family budget and redirect investments, but there's still no way you can fund your dream. The money just isn't there. We need you to hear this: there's no such thing as hopelessness. After almost four decades of helping people find ways to achieve their dreams, we have found that a high percentage of our clients can fund their business vehicles.

Yes, sometimes funding a business requires out-of-the-box thinking. And it will definitely require a steadfast commitment to your dream and the courage to move beyond the "yeah, but" phase, where thoughts, such as *yeah, but those other people had money* or *yeah, but I don't have any equity in my home and I lost a ton of money on my retirement plan,* distract you from focusing on your future.

We won't allow you to dismiss your possibilities or give up on your dream because you believe your circumstances are unique. Just like the other fears and barriers you may have encountered along this path, the money question is one that can be dealt with and overcome.

PREPARING FOR THE TRANSITION

Funding is a major issue for many people, not because money is difficult to find, but because most people are not aware of all the options that exist.

Often, *funding*—one of the looming F-words—seems like the insurmountable barrier to self-sufficiency. A key element of the coaching is to help clients shift their mindsets and the paradigm of fear associated with funding. One of our goals is to help our clients view funding as an empowering part of the coaching experience. It is not something to fear but to embrace.

So how do you get beyond funding fears?

The answer is in your Career Capital—in essence, everything you have done up to this point in your life. Think about everything you bring to the table, including your work ethic and your transferable skills. The key is leverage. How can you leverage your experiences? How can you best leverage your assets—your retirement plans, other investments, savings, and real estate—everything that gives you net worth to fund your future Income, Lifestyle, Wealth, and Equity? Your family and friends can also provide a source of funding, so think about who can help you.

In today's new normal, many people have shifted into a scarcity mentality. Too many people haven't been producing any income or haven't been producing at the levels they once did. As a result, they're fearful of using their career capital, because they aren't looking at the return on that investment, just at the risk of depleting their financial resources.

Although the instinctive reaction in many cases is to not spend that capital on a business like a franchise, in truth, you are not *spending* your career capital on anything. When you invest in financing a business, you are moving your assets from one line item to another—turning it from a reactive investment into a proactive one, but your net worth has not diminished.

Reactive investments are a roller coaster at best, and most people are tired of the bumpy ride. We believe that, in many cases, franchise ownership can be used as a vehicle to empower people and give them the confidence they need to seize their destiny and create a future with better Income, Lifestyle, Wealth, and Equity.

Give yourself permission to learn and find out from people who have invested their money directly themselves. As part of your Journey of Discovery with The Entrepreneur's Source, your Career Ownership Coach will introduce you to people who have made the leap. You will be able to ask questions so you can learn more. As you explore your options, we encourage you to ask whether those people are happy with their ROI and if they would choose the same vehicle again.

Remember John, the man about to retire, whom we met in an earlier chapter? He has spent his entire career building his pension and setting aside money in his savings account. Although he knows that his careful planning has not left him quite enough for his retirement years, he worries about spending his savings and 401(k) on a franchise.

What if the business fails? How will he survive if this latest investment doesn't work out? As John goes through our coaching journey and starts gathering information and understanding what it takes to go from unemployment to employment, he realizes that he isn't spending money but simply reallocating funds to invest in himself—going from reactive to proactive investments.

To escape that scarcity mentality, you need to look back at your career achievements, everything you have made up your mind to do and at which you have been successful. Imagine what would happen if you moved those financial and emotional investments from reactive to proactive, investing in yourself instead of in someone else's profit. When seen from that vantage point, isn't it more of a risk not to invest in your future?

KNOW YOUR OPTIONS

One of the most prevalent misconceptions about funding is that there is only one way to do it. We seem to hear how difficult it is for most people to find a loan, but as with so many other things today, the traditional paths are no longer the only—or the best—way to accomplish things.

THERE'S NO TIME LIKE THE PRESENT

Even when banks and other financial institutions go through periods during which they are more stringent in lending money, businesses and franchises still get funded. We have seen this in up economic times and down economic times. There never seems to be a wrong time to start a business. The key again is mindset and resilience, as Henry Ford's famous quote goes, "Whether you think you can, or you think you can't—you're right."

Just as with every other aspect of discovery, the key to finding funding is in educating yourself on the options available to you. We have the resources to help you with that exploration. In many cases, you do not have to rely on a single source of funding and can look to multiple avenues to achieve your financing.

In addition to your Career Capital, sometimes franchise business models are willing and able to offer financing or leasing options. Or maybe part of the funding package for a brick-and-mortar business includes leasehold improvements and equipment. What you will undoubtedly learn is that there are numerous funding sources beyond traditional avenues. It is simply a matter of exploration.

Decisions, Decisions, Decisions

It's time now to look at the other obstacle that can often creep up even after you have reached a point of clarity about what the best road ahead may be: indecision.

The fear of making a wrong or a bad decision prevents far too many from pursuing their dreams or from even exploring possibilities. Living with the consequences of a poor decision seems like too great a risk. Rather than making a bad or wrong decision, they refuse to make a move. In essence, however, they are choosing to remain in a situation that no longer serves them—which is a bad decision.

We have designed our Journey of Discovery experience to help people reach a point of clarity where they realize they have gathered enough information and find themselves beyond the decision-making point. The right decision becomes so evident that not making it is clearly a bad choice. You, too, will know when you have reached that point.

From time to time, however, people suffer from what we call "paralysis by analysis." They continue searching for facts and information, even when deep inside they know they don't need any more data. The true cause of this condition is that they are looking for a 100 percent guarantee when there is no guarantee or feeling 100 percent comfortable when that feeling may remain elusive because the situation is new and different to them.

If you experience paralysis by analysis, your coach will help you review the information you have gathered against what you have defined as your vision for your future and your goals. Beyond that, the only remedy is action.

There will be times when we have to accept that nobody can always make the right decision. All we can do is explore the options, make an informed choice, and then start working at making that choice the right decision.

"It's easier to act your way into a new way of thinking than think your way into a new way of acting."[27]
—Jerry Sternin

ALL YOU NEED IS (A LITTLE) TIME

When people come to The Entrepreneur's Source for coaching, many assume the experience will take a tremendous amount of time, especially in narrowing down their possibilities. Some even use that assumption as an excuse not to take the Journey of Discovery, claiming they do not have the time. It is kind of like saying, "I am too busy to develop healthier eating habits." If you are waiting for the perfect time, it will probably never arrive. We emphasize holding our clients accountable for their goals, helping them stay focused on achieving their potential during a career change, and becoming the best version of themselves. You need to know, however, that if you come to us for coaching, you're the one who sets the pace. At a minimum, we will encourage you to do or learn one thing a day about what it will take to go from unemployment, underemployment, or even employment to empowerment.

You are the only person who can decide the outcome of the next chapter of your life. Your ambitions and goals are up to you, as is the path you choose to achieve them. We're here to get you thinking and to lead you as you navigate the opportunities of your career transition. The rest is up to you.

This Journey of Discovery accommodates even the busiest work, life, or travel schedule. You will typically meet for an hour or so a week with your coach, almost always virtually, by phone or video conference.

The time needed to reach a point of clarity varies from person to person. You cannot force discovery, and like an insight, you never quite know when it is going to hit you. But if you stick with the journey, you will reach that point of clarity, when you know exactly what you must do to take charge of creating your ideal future. As we said earlier in this chapter, this is not a fear-free state, but it is a state of confidence when you push through the fear to make your dreams a reality.

Trust the process. Do the work. And give yourself time and freedom to explore your options. You will find the clarity you need to take the next step.

CHAPTER 7

CASE STUDIES THAT CLARIFY

The byproduct of a new future can also be a new business and new life

You make a new life by making new choices.
—Sean Stephenson

B y now, you have read about what you need to do to discover your path to your desired Income, Lifestyle, Wealth, Equity, and your YOU 2.0. You have a good idea of what is involved with The Entrepreneur's Source Journey of Discovery.

Now we want to show you what it's like to go through this journey from beginning to end with the help of some real-life examples. All names and identifying details have been changed to protect the privacy of our clients, but the journey they went through will allow you to envision yourself going through similar steps.

KEVIN'S STORY

Public relations executive Kevin came to The Entrepreneur's Source after deciding that he was dissatisfied with his current high-paying ad firm job. At fifty years of age, he had three kids heading for college and a wife whose job didn't earn enough to support the family on its own. At Kevin's first coaching session, his Career Ownership Coach asked him to give a brief sketch of his job—what he liked about it, what he hated, and what motivated him to seek out other options.

It was at that point that Kevin began his Journey of Discovery. During the next several weeks, he took a closer look at his life and job and tried to identify the reasons he was contemplating a change. Like many people, Kevin found the soul-searching experience difficult. Using the tools that his Career Ownership Coach provided, Kevin was able to crystallize what he desired in his life.

Kevin was not able to pinpoint the reasons for his dissatisfaction immediately. However, the more he thought about it, the more he realized he was tired of the long business trips, the time he missed out on spending with his family, and the continual worry that no matter how good he was at his job or how many hours he put in with his company, he would eventually, like so many of his friends had in recent years, get a pink slip.

In short, he was tired of feeling like he had no control over his life and being forced to work so hard for what, at the end of the day, was someone else's dream.

As Kevin imagined what his future might hold five years down the line, he dreamt of a career that challenged him creatively and intellectually. He wanted to be free to go to his son's football game without worrying or hurrying back to the office for yet another interminable conference call. He pictured himself running his own business and controlling his destiny.

Kevin considered how those closest to him would react to his new goals. Knowing his wife's income wouldn't cover the family's expenses, he worried about what she would say. This Journey of Discovery awakened internal dreams and he felt new life for the first time in a long time.

It wasn't like he was disconnected from reality. He knew very well that they had a mortgage and many other bills, not to mention their kids' college tuition. How would his wife react if Kevin told her he considered options outside the traditional career path, especially if some of those options meant the family budget might take a temporary hit?

When he finally shared his hopes and dreams with his wife, Kevin found she shared many of his fears. Without the benefit of having experienced the coaching sessions, she could only see the obstacles and risks threatening her family. Kevin's paradigm, however, had shifted. He could picture the future he had always wanted.

Understanding that his mindset shift was the result of the coaching, Kevin invited his wife and family to get involved in the experience. Going on the Journey of Discovery together, they used one another as sounding boards and were able to discuss their feelings. After all, a change in Kevin's career would impact them all, especially if he started a business.

KEVIN'S YOU 2.0

Creating his YOU 2.0 caused Kevin to reflect on some thought-provoking questions. As he contemplated the dangers facing him and his family in the future, he realized that many of them were concerns and obstacles commonly experienced by people embarking on new and different career paths.

Although one of his primary worries was that his hard-earned skills wouldn't be transferable to a new job, Kevin's biggest anxiety involved his age. At fifty years old, Kevin had been working in public relations for decades, but he knew that many companies wanted to hire younger employees at lower salaries. If he were to leave his current job, he knew it would be unlikely for another company to hire a man nearing retirement age.

Once Kevin had taken the time to address his concerns, he was prompted by his coach to talk and write about his desires for the future. As he did so, he found that earning enough to pay for his children's education while still being able to build the wealth and equity that could support his wife and him after they retired was very important to him. They had always talked about traveling more once their work years were behind them, and Kevin wanted to make sure they could still live out those dreams. He knew that in his present job, that dream was becoming more and more unreachable.

Finally, Kevin documented his strengths. As an ad executive, he was creative, organized, and deadline oriented. He was great with clients and developed a large network of friends and colleagues in both the business world and his community. Although Kevin worried that some of his skills would not transfer well into a new career, his coach introduced him to tools that allowed him to see just how valuable those skills and traits could be in any industry.

By the end of his Journey of Discovery, Kevin felt much better about what he had to offer and which skills would help him on his new career path. He felt all of the expected fear and anxiety but worked through those feelings and decided not to make decisions based on emotion but rather on fact, and started down the road towards greater Income, Lifestyle, Wealth, and Equity.

JOHN'S STORY

Nearing retirement age, John was concerned his Social Security and pension were going to dry up. He and his wife wanted to travel and enjoy their retirement years, but John knew that, without his usual paycheck, the dreams of travel didn't look too promising. Having heard from a friend about how our unique coaching experience helps people work on their vision of their future and explore actionable opportunities, he decided to meet with a Career Ownership Coach and explore what options existed for him after he retired from his current job.

During the first session, John's coach asked John about his picture of the future. "Well," John began, "My wife and I have spent our entire lives working and raising our kids. We have always said we want to travel more, and now might be our last chance to do it. I am not getting any younger, and I want to make sure that, after I retire, I will have enough money to keep some of my lifestyle, travel, and maybe save some money for the grandkids."

His Career Ownership Coach pointed out that working on his YOU 2.0 gives him a pathway on how to make all of this doable. John, however, was not as certain.

"I'm not looking for another full-time job—that is why I am retiring—but I need something more than just my pension. At my age, what kind of options am I looking at?"

John's coach asked him a question, inspired by Dan Sullivan, the co-founder of Strategic Coach.

"If we looked at your life a year from today, what has to have happened during that period, both personally and professionally, for you to be happy with your progress?"

The answer to this question is intricately related to YOU 2.0. John's coach helped him to see, saying, "Once you're certain you have explored all your options and have a better idea of where you want to end up in five years' time, we look at some possibilities and learn whether they have the potential to get you where you want to go."

As the sessions went on, with the assistance of his coach, John clarified what he wanted more of in his life. He created a vision of what his new life would look like after retirement. He saw brand new possibilities. In time, his coach introduced John to a few business models.

"But I don't know anything about these industries," John said. "I mean, I don't even like kids! How can I own and operate a haircutting franchise for kids? None of these businesses are right for me."

"Before you make any decisions," his coach reminded him, "Talk to some of their franchisees. See how they've made these businesses work for them. I'd be curious to hear what you learn about their motivations."

Unconvinced but open to learning, John gave his coach the benefit of the doubt. Joined by his wife, he educated himself on each model, talked to the franchisees, and got a better feeling for these businesses as vehicles rather than as an extension of the career he was about to leave.

One of the things he learned that intrigued him about the haircutting franchise was that the other business owners were not hairstylists either nor did they come from that industry. He also learned that many of them had multiple locations, which they were running semi-absentee. They had hired managers to oversee the day-to-day operations.

Just as he narrowed down his possibilities—homing in on the kids' haircare franchise, of all things—John's doubts re-emerged. The company he worked for offered him a role as a consultant. Although he was tempted to take the opportunity, John realized that the job with his old company was not as secure as he would like to believe. And it certainly did not have any wealth-building opportunity associated with it. Besides, at a decreased salary level, and with the sporadic nature of consulting work, it simply didn't give him the Income, Lifestyle, Wealth, and Equity he knew he needed to live the future he envisioned.

At some point, John asked his coach and the franchisor for more details about the new business owner training sessions for the haircare franchise. Without even realizing it, he had moved beyond the decision-making phase. He was ready to seize the future he had always wanted.

BETH'S STORY

"Look," corporate executive Beth began her session with her Career Ownership Coach. "My current job just is not working for me anymore. I make a great salary, sure, but I see more of the airport than my house. I need something different, something that lets me keep my current income, but allows me to have more free time and less travel."

Her coach listened intently.

"A friend of mine went through your program and is doing great, so I thought I might give it a try. Just let me know how much I need to invest."

Listening to what Beth was hoping to get out of a new career path, her coach assured her he doesn't charge for his time, and other than some books or educational programs he may recommend, the biggest investment is her commitment to remain open to learning new things.

He continued, "This experience is about exploration and education. It is just as much about figuring out what you want your future to look like as it is about finding the business that will work for you."

"But I already know what I want, and I've done all the research on the latest business models out there. I just need you to tell me what the sure-fire industries and investments are."

"There are no guarantees here," her coach explained. "Our Journey of Discovery is designed to help you explore your goals, needs, and expectations and to allow you to gain clarity about what you want the next version of you to look like, your YOU 2.0. We then look at business models that make sense as vehicles that serve your life's purpose. Ninety-five percent of our clients who end up in a business, choose one they admittedly would have never looked at on their own or had previously dismissed. This statistic surprises many of our clients."[28]

The coach piqued Beth's interest and she engaged him as her coach. Through working on her YOU 2.0, by defining her Income, Lifestyle, Wealth, and Equity expectations, she realized the solution she needed would not come from chasing the latest job trend. Instead, she seriously examined her current situation and goals for her future. She eventually came to the conclusion she wanted to be self-sufficient. She wanted to do something for herself and take control of her life and destiny.

As a single woman, she did not have a family to question her decisions. Nonetheless, her friends and coworkers were stunned when she told them that she would leave her stable corporate job to pursue the path to self-sufficiency. They fired off questions: "What about your paycheck and 401(k)?" "Do you know the statistics on the rate of failure for small businesses?"

As she listened to their concerns, doubt set in. It grew after seeing the business models her coach presented. None of them seemed even remotely connected to her area of expertise. How would her skills transfer into any of these industries? If she embarked on one of these business models and failed, how would she ever re-enter the corporate world at her current job level and salary?

"What if you looked at the models as vehicles and not an extension of your current career," her coach asked. "Be careful not to fall into the trap of buying yourself a job. Instead, think about how you can use this new business as a way of achieving the flexibility and long-term wealth you said you wanted. I am sure you are not the only person who has had this concern. Why don't you speak to a few more people who have taken the leap? Remember, feeling nervous about embarking on something new is normal. On the other side, getting uncomfortable in the short term to experience long-term success might be a tradeoff worth taking.

Beth did some soul-searching. She looked past the false security of the corporate world and beyond the fads that she thought she needed. She found a path that helped her achieve her desired lifestyle while increasing her wealth and equity.

DOUG'S STORY

After running across The Entrepreneur's Source online, recent college graduate Doug faced a completely different set of challenges.

"With all of the loans I had to take out to finish school, I'm already up to my eyeballs in debt, and I'm not even twenty-eight years old," Doug explained. "I majored in business so I could land a great job after I graduated, but it has only been two years, and I've already had to change jobs three times. I can't even propose to my girlfriend because I do not have any savings. How can I think about being self-sufficient when I can barely make my monthly loan payments?"

His Career Ownership Coach heard Doug's desperation and said, "It sounds like we've met for a reason. Maybe it's time for you to work on the next version of yourself. Are you ready to explore what YOU 2.0 could look like? If so, I will work with you under one condition. You need to promise to keep an open mind. You can't make any premature decisions. And if you do, then do I have your permission to point that out? Know this, I will have you explore some options other than the ones your college career counselor exposed you to."

For the first time in a long time, Doug felt a tinge of hope. "I don't have any problems exploring some different options.

And I think I can be pretty open-minded about whatever you show me, but I am worried I might be too young to start thinking about becoming self-sufficient. Shouldn't I pay my dues first?"

"That's a common worry," his coach confirmed. "But we aren't living in your parents' job market. Do you feel college prepared you to be financially independent and have a successful career? Do you feel what worked for your parents' generation is going to work for you? Do you believe that is the best pathway to achieve what you really want? Is paying your dues in the corporate world going to get you where you want to go?"

Doug processed these questions and his coach continued. "Many of our clients, young and old, find that taking charge of their careers is the best way to get them where they want to go. They discover they do not want to continue to work on somebody else's dream. They want to work on their own dreams. The fact you get to contemplate and learn about all your possibilities at this point in your life and career is truly a blessing. I have many clients who would have loved to have found the road to self-sufficiency at your age. Remember, I am not asking you to make any decisions right now. What I am asking of you is to keep an open mind and educate yourself about all your options."

In the end, Doug concluded his coach was right. What does he have to lose? He only had insights to gain. He chose to embark on the Journey of Discovery. It may go against everything he was taught, but it turned out this was the direction he needed to pursue to follow his dream.

EMILY'S STORY

When Emily was introduced to her coach, her biggest concern was providing for her two children.

"I have a stable job and a paycheck," she told her coach. "But I never have any time to spend with my kids. All my energy goes into my work, and I feel like I am missing watching them grow up. I am a single mom, and I just want something that will give me enough money to provide for my son and daughter without making me sacrifice my time with them."

Emily's coach heard her concerns. He listened before responding. "Our mission is to help you see a way to achieve your Income, Lifestyle, Wealth, and Equity goals."

He explained the Journey of Discovery and the power of creating a vision statement. He unpacked how the YOU 2.0 worksheet helped define goals and how, if, and when they got there, they would learn about different business models.

"Wait a minute." Emily stopped her coach the moment she heard about the business models. "Owning my own business? There's no way I could do that."

She believed it would require even more time than her current job.

Emily shared her concerns. "I could have fewer conference calls and meetings, but running a business could tie me up with more administrative tasks. And what if the business fails? I may have to put in a ton of hours right now, but at least I have a steady paycheck coming in."

Her coach heard the concern in her voice. He replied, "I can certainly understand your concerns about what it takes to run your own business. What if you were to find out that there are other people in similar situations to yours that have been able to achieve what you say you want? Would it make a difference? What if you were to find out that your knee-jerk reaction is false evidence appearing real? I am not trying to sell you a business or even convince you that business ownership is right for you. I am, however, inviting you on a Journey of Discovery that allows you to educate yourself about the possibilities that exist, so you can create a better future for yourself and your family.

"My role as a coach is simply to ask questions and challenge you on limiting beliefs that may be holding you back from the life you say you want. There are many misconceptions about the time it takes to run your own business. But as your coach, I represent your interest first and foremost. I serve clients who have similar concerns to the ones you've raised all the time," the coach reassured Emily.

"I can understand your concern about leaving the security of a corporate paycheck. Are you ever concerned that it may go away? Could layoffs ever happen? What about the possibility of your company merging or downsizing? Many of my clients face these concerns and feel let down by their jobs. That is why I urge everybody to, at the very least, educate themselves. Learn about the possibilities that exist for you and your family and then do what is right and makes the most sense for your situation."

After she listened to her coach, Emily took an honest look at her current career and decided to embark on her Journey of Discovery. Once she did, sure enough, she realized many of her assumptions about the security of the corporate world changed. Although she had a steady paycheck at the moment, she knew that situation could change in an instant. She realized she was working to increase someone else's Income, Lifestyle, Wealth, and Equity, while never getting the opportunity to build those things for herself and her children.

Guided by her coach, Emily explored options outside her comfort zone and started to see that she owed it to her son and daughter to muster the courage and fight the fear she felt. She needed to take the opportunity to build a future for all of them—one where she didn't have to give up attending her son's parent-teacher night or her daughter's recital just to make ends meet.

In these five examples, the clients coming to The Entrepreneur's Source had different backgrounds and motivations. Your Journey of Discovery will be just as unique to you and your life. It is your journey. Regardless of who you are and where you came from, however, choose today not to allow your past to determine your future.

You have the power to determine your Income, your Lifestyle, your Wealth, and your Equity. The vehicles to get there may not have been the ones that initially came to mind. You are courageous for keeping an open mind and challenging your current perceptions. In time, you will be rewarded.

NEXT STEPS

GROWTH IS A NEVER-ENDING JOURNEY

Life isn't static, your future shouldn't be either.

Never stop learning. Never stop growing.
—Paula Walker Baker

Everything was fine—until it wasn't.

Imagine boarding a plane wearing your flip-flops after a trip to the Bahamas. Although you had an amazing time, part of you is excited to go home and get back to life as normal.

One minute the pilot said he wasn't feeling well, and the next he slumped over the controls of the single-engine plane, sending it into a nosedive.[29]

Not what you were expecting. So, what do you do? What does anyone do in an unplanned event like this?

This was the exact scenario Darren Harrison and one other passenger experienced in the Cessna 208.

According to *NBC News*, "Despite having no flying experience, Harrison climbed over three rows of seats into the cockpit, moved the pilot out of his seat, and scrambled to put on a pair of headphones and make contact with air traffic control—all as the plane was heading down."[30]

His audio from a call he made to air traffic control at Fort Pierce tower, said it all: "I've got a serious situation here. My pilot has gone incoherent. I have no idea how to fly the airplane."

ASK FOR HELP

Harrison didn't ignore the situation at hand. Although the other passenger may have been paralyzed with fear, Harrison took imperfect action and asked for help.

At first, Harrison didn't know where the aircraft even was. But with aid from air traffic controllers, he found his bearings. His coach on the ground gave clear instructions.

The *NBC News* report noted, "The flight instructor, Robert 'Bobby' Morgan, told Harrison, 'You look great; you're a little fast; what I want you to do is grab the throttle. Just pull that back a little bit because we need you (to) be slowed down.'"

The story was picked up by media from around the world. CNN reported, "'He was really calm,' Morgan said. "He said, 'I don't know how to fly. I don't know how to stop this thing if I do get on the runway.'"[31]

CNN shared more dialogue between Harrison and his new coach, Morgan. "Try to hold the wings level and see if you can start descending for me. Push forward on the controls and descend at a very slow rate," the air traffic controller could be heard telling the fledgling pilot in LiveATC audio.

A SAFE LANDING

Morgan made the key decision to guide the aircraft to the area's biggest airport, helping the passenger-turned-pilot position his aircraft eight miles out from Palm Beach International, "just so he could just have a really big target to aim at."

Together, they got the Cessna to touch down on the runway. Footage obtained by CNN affiliate WPBF showed Harrison's successful first attempt at landing, a feat that takes about twenty hours to learn with typical flight instruction. The landing rated ten out of ten, in Morgan's view.

"I felt like I was going to cry then because I had so much adrenaline built up," Morgan said. "I was really happy that it worked out and that nobody got hurt."

Other pilots were stunned, as another air traffic controller relayed across the airwaves what had just unfolded, other audio captured by LiveATC.net indicates.

"You just witnessed a couple of passengers land that plane," the tower operator can be heard telling an American Airlines pilot waiting to take off for Charlotte, North Carolina. "Did you say the passengers landed the airplane?" the American Airlines pilot asked. "Oh, my God. Great job," he said.

Don't Fly Solo

You probably know from experience that life often interrupts well-laid plans. Harrison had no plans to become a pilot. He was quite comfortable being a passenger. Thankfully, his coach helped him land safely.

This story might be a metaphor for your life. Perhaps before reading this book, you were coasting through life, oblivious to the new adventures that lay ahead of you.

Maybe you were quite comfortable being an employee. Maybe the employee mindset was something you adopted over the years, and you've been content to let someone else's dream dictate your income and schedule.

The truth is, we're all pilots. We all have the responsibility to land our planes safely. But make no mistake: No one needs to fly solo. Just like Harrison discovered, a confident coach is an invaluable asset.

Hopefully, this book has opened your mind to what's possible. Creating your new future is a creative and collaborative process.

Don't fly solo. We're here to help. We'll coach you on how to arrive safely at your intended destination.

On that topic, let's return to the first question we asked way back in the introduction: "What do you want to be when you grow up?"

If the trajectory of your current career path makes you feel like you want to revolt, remember that you don't need to have all the answers right now. All you need to do is give yourself permission to reimagine and reclaim the life of your dreams. From there, all you have to do is follow your Journey of Discovery until the path becomes clear. We're here for you every step of the way.

APPENDICES

5 Steps to Uncovering Your Primary Aim with the Help of The Entrepreneur's Source

Use this next section to prime the pump and get the thoughts flowing about what you want.

What is your Primary Aim in life?

If you feel fulfilled and that you're living life with purpose, then you have found your Primary Aim. Your Primary Aim is your innermost driving force—it is what gives you a sense of direction and purpose. It motivates you to your highest level of energy and sustains you over the long haul. Your Primary Aim is the source of the vitality, commitment, and vision you need to get the most out of your life and your career.

The vast majority of individuals aren't in touch with their Primary Aim. It's there, within all of us, but most of us simply haven't taken the time to identify it. Some of us may even avoid it because we know we would then be compelled to execute it. Your Primary Aim is a matter of discovery, not invention. You don't create your Primary Aim; it already exists within you.

Are you looking to uncover your Primary Aim so you can actively shape your life and career rather than passively accept whatever joy and pain happen to come your way? Let's review the five steps of uncovering your Primary Aim so you can start playing an active role in shaping your future, creating your happiness, and experiencing success.

THE 5 STEPS TO FINDING YOUR PRIMARY AIM

For most of us, the journey to uncover our Primary Aim involves finding new ways of looking at ourselves and our lives. It answers questions about our core values, beliefs, and dreams. It requires you to look inward and get in touch with your feelings to guide you to find what truly is important to you.

To start getting in tune with uncovering your Primary Aim, follow these five steps:

1. **Identify what you don't want**. Begin by creating a list of what you don't want any longer in your life. Once you're done listing all of these items, read through your list carefully and be aware of the feelings that each specific item brings up. Circle the items (narrow it down to one to six items) that trigger the strongest negative emotions for you.

2. **Recognize what you do want**. Next, create the opposite list of what you did in step one. Start writing down the elements that you do want in your life. Stay away from material things and money and instead focus on non-tangible items. Once you've completed your list, read through and circle the items (narrow it down to one to six items) you most want to be a part of your life and that bring the strongest feelings of happiness.

3. **Prioritize and break barriers**. Create a new list of these most-important items from your "do" list and rank them from the most important to the least impor- tant. Read through each item and brainstorm the barriers that get in the way of you achieving them.

Write these barriers down next to the item. This step will help you better visualize and prioritize how you can achieve these goals. It's important to be aware of limiting beliefs.

4. **Write your eulogy**. This may feel a little strange at first but think of the far-off day in your future when you're gone, and all of your friends and family are assembled at your memorial. What do you want your eulogy to say? Write down what you wish others remembered you for and what others said about you once you're gone.

5. **Assemble your Primary Aim**. Write a statement of the essence of your Primary Aim. This should be a single sentence that describes what you want your life to be like for it to express what's most important to you. It should make you feel energized, enthusiastic, and committed. Keep re-writing until your final statement makes you feel this way.

Congratulations! After following these five steps, you should have established your Primary Aim.

Uncovering your Primary Aim is the first step in moving from an employment mindset to an empowerment mindset. Once your Primary Aim is uncovered, it's time to bring it to life! This is where a coach can be of great benefit. A Career Ownership Coach at The Entrepreneur's Source is like your personal guide for your Journey of Discovery. A coach doesn't provide all of the answers to you, he or she asks the questions to facilitate the process of self-discovery. For assistance in getting started on your new career path, reach out and get connected to a Career Ownership Coach at The Entrepreneur's Source: EntrepreneursSource.com.

QUESTIONS TO STIMULATE YOUR THINKING ABOUT YOUR PRIMARY AIM

- What do you want your life to look and feel like?
- What do you value most? What's important to you?
- What matters most at this point in your life?
- What would you like to be able to say about your life after it's too late to do anything about it?
- Many years from now, at your funeral, what do you hope will be said about you in your eulogy?
- How do you want your life to feel on a day-to-day basis?
- What would you like people's perceptions of you to be?
- What are your daydreams about?
- When you were young, what did you want to be when you grew up?
- Do you ever find yourself wishing you were different?
- What do you wish? Why aren't you that way? What gets in your way?
- Of all the things you have done in your life, what has given you the most satisfaction or pleasure?
- Of all the things you have done in your life, what has given you the least satisfaction or pleasure?
- If you no longer had to work, how would you spend your time? And with whom?
- What is missing from your life? When you find yourself wishing for something, what is it?
- What motivates you to perform above and beyond the call of duty?
- What are your greatest strengths?
- What are your greatest weaknesses?
- What do you want to achieve but find impossible to do? What barriers make it impossible? Think again; are those barriers really insurmountable?

- Where is your professional future headed?
- Are you on track?
- Will your current path take you where you want to go?
- What would happen if you started spending all those hours doing something for yourself?
- What would your life look like? What would you do if failure were not an option?
- Do you tend to take the path of least resistance and avoid looking at yourself and take responsibility for your life and future?
- Do you close yourself to possibilities just because you have never considered them before?
- Are you afraid of change?
- How would you describe your feelings about your present career?
- What do you want more of in your life, personally and professionally?
- What do you want less of in your life, personally and professionally?
- Five years from now, if you stay on your current career path, how do you see yourself achieving financial independence?
- What are your biggest concerns about changing careers?
- If you knew you couldn't fail, what career would you choose?
- If we looked at your life a year from today, what has to have happened during that period, both personally and professionally, for you to be happy with your progress?

In your present job:

- Are you feeling under-appreciated?
- How about feeling left out of important decisions or stymied by bureaucratic flab?

- Are you in a dead-end job, waiting your turn for that pink slip?
- Do you ever feel you could do great things if you could run the show?
- What do you worry about?
- What makes you afraid?
- What causes anxiety for you?
- What keeps you away from making a change?
- What makes you run the other way when someone brings it up?
- Are you even aware of all the voices of fear and all of its disguises?

NOTES

1. Grace Dean and Madison Hoff. "Nearly three-quarters of workers are actively thinking about quitting their job, according to a recent survey." October 7, 2021, https://www.businessinsider.com/great-resignation-labor-shortage-workers-thinking-about-quitting-joblist-report-2021-10.
2. S. von Stumm, B. Hell, and T. Chamorro-Premuzic. "The Hungry Mind: Intellectual Curiosity Is the Third Pillar of Academic Performance." *Perspectives on Psychological Science*, 2011; 6 (6): 574 DOI:10.1177/1745691611421204, accessed September 13, 2022, https://www.sciencedaily.com/releases/2011/10/111027150211.htm.
3. "Is Intelligence Correlated with Curiosity?" *FutureLearn. Com.*, accessed September 13, 2022, https://www.futurelearn.com/info/courses/developing curiosity/0/steps/156372.
4. Friedman, Zach. "Shock Poll: 7 In 10 Americans Live Paycheck to Paycheck." *Forbes.* February 8, 2022, https://www.forbes.com/sites/zackfriedman/2022/02/08/shock-poll-7-in-10-americans-live-pay-check-to-pay-check/ ?sh=4f07d01a55f6.
5. "Gen Z and Gen Alpha Infographic Update," accessed September 13, 2022, https://mccrindle.com.au/insights/blogarchive/Gen-z-and-gen-alpha-infographic-update/.

6. Robert Frost, et al. *The Road Not Taken: A Selection of Robert Frost's Poems* (New York: H. Holt and Co, 1991).

7. *The Matrix*, directed by Wachowski, Lana, and Lilly Wachowski (Warner Bros. Studios, 1999).

8. "Revolt," accessed September 13, 2022, https://www. google.com/search?q=revolt+meaning&rlz1C1GCEA_en US891US891&oq=revolt+meaning&aqs=chrome69i57j 0i512l9.2967j0j4&sourceid=chrome&ie=UTF-8.

9. Miller, G.E. "The U.S. is the Most Overworked Developed Nation in the World." *20SomethingFinance. Com.* January 30, 2022, https://20somethingfinance. com/20somethingfinance.com/American-hours-worked productivity-vacation/.

10. Terry Powell, "Entrepreneur's Source Terry Powell Says Entrepreneurs Start with Asking 'Why'," n.d., https://en-trepreneurssource.com/blog/e-source-says/entrepreneurs-source-terry-powell-says-entrepreneurs-start asking/.

11. Thomas Jefferson quote. "If you want you never had . . .", accessed September 13, 2022, https://www.monticello.org/ research-education/thomas-jefferson-encyclopedia/if-you-want-something-you-have-never-had-spurious-quotation/.

12. Terry Powell, "Entrepreneur's Source Franchise Infographic Examines Employment vs. Business Ownership," n.d., https://entrepreneurssource.com/blog/ trends in franchising/entrepreneurs-source-franchise-infographic-examines-employment-vs-business-ownership/.

13. Wikipedia. "Goal." *Wikipedia,* accessed September 13, 2022, https://en.wikipedia.org/wiki/Goal.

14. Wikipedia. "Need." *Wikipedia,* accessed September 13, 2022, https://en.wikipedia.org/wiki/Need.

15. Michelle Singletary, "Your pension plan benefits may not be as ironclad as you think." *The Washington Post.*

September 9, 2019, https://www.washingtonpost.com/business/2019/09/09/ your-pension-plan-benefits-may-not-be-as-ironclad-as-you-think.

16. Emily Brandon, "10 Jobs That Still Offer Traditional Pensions." *U.S. News and World Report.* March 14, 2022, https://money. Usnews.com/money/retirement/baby-boomers/slideshows/jobs-that-still-offer-traditional-pensions.

17. G.E. Miller, "Does your 401K Match Up Against the Averages?" *20SometingFinance.com.* January 7, 2022, https://20somethingfinance.com/401k-match.

18. Darren Kelsey, "Comment: Prince Harry saga: what advice would Carl Jung give?" New Castle University: Press Office. May 28, 2021, https://www.ncl.ac.uk/press/articles/archive/2021/05/conversationprinceharry/#:~:text=Jung%20once%20said%3A%20%E2%80%9Cthe%20greatest, influence%20us%20later%20in%20life.

19. Dan Sullivan, "How to Sell Transformation Using The One Question." *The Multiplier Mindset Blog,* accessed, September 13, 2022, https://resources.strategic-coach.com/the-multiplier-mindset-blog/how-to-sell-transformation-using-this-one-question

20. G.E. Miller, "70% of Americans want to be Self-Employed. What is Stopping you?" February 13, 2022, https://20somethingfinance.com/self-employment-poll.

21. "FACT SHEET: President Biden Announces Student Loan Relief for Borrowers Who Need It Most." *Whitehouse.gov.* August 24, 2022, https://www.whitehouse.gov/ briefing-room/statements-releases/2022/08/24/fact-sheet-president-biden-announces-student-loan- relief-for-borrowers-who-need-it-most.

22. Brittne Kakulla, "Lifelong Learning Older Adults for Personal Growth and Cognitive Health." *AARP.org.* March 2022. https://www.aarp.org/research/topics/life/

info-2022/lifelong-learning-older-adults.html.

23. John Wooden quote, "It's what you learn . . .", accessed September 13, 2022, https://www.quoteam-bition.com/john-wooden-quotes.

24. Melinda Emerson, "Taking Your Small Business to the Next Level w/ Michael Gerber." *Succeedas YourOwnBoss. com.* April 22, 2010

25. Emerson, "Taking Your Small Business," April 22, 2010.

26. Shunryu Suzuki, *Zen Mind, Beginner's Mind: Informal Talks on Zen Meditation and Practice* (Tokyo: Weatherhill, 1970).

27. Richard Pascale, Jerry Sternin, and Monique Sternin. *The Power of Positive Deviance: How Unlikely Innovators Solve the World's Toughest Problems* (Boston, MA: Harvard Business Review Press, 2010

28. Powell, "Entrepreneur's Source," https://entrepreneurs-source.com/blog/trends-in-franchising/entrepreneurs-source-franchise-infographic-examines-employment-vs-business-ownership/.

29. Becky Sullivan. "A passenger makes an emergency airplane landing in Florida." *NPR.org.* May 11, 2022, https://www.npr.org/2022/05/11/1098313826/passenger-makes-emergency-airplane-landing-florida.

30. Marlene Lenthang. "How a passenger with no flight experience landed a plane in a nosedive after the pilot passed out." *NBCNews. com.* May 12, 2022, https://www.nbcnews.com/news/us-news/ passenger-no-flight-experience-saved-plane- nosedive-landed-pilot-passe-rcna28492.

31. Jamiel Lynch, Dakin Andone, and Pete Muntean. "A passenger with no flying experience landed a plane at a Florida airport after the pilot became incapacitated." May 11, 2022, https://www.cnn.com/travel/article/florida-passenger-lands-plane/index.html.

BACK ADS

Find Your Event

visit our EVENT page that showcases all 100+ coaches' events across the USA and Canada.

https://entrepreneurssource.com/events/

Blog:

A Trusted Resource for Your Career Revolution

The Entrepreneur's Source Blog is your One-Stop for Career-Ownership Content.

Exclusive Insights. Helpful Hints. Best Practices

EntrepreneursSource.com/blog/

Podcast:

Tune in to the top career-ownership podcast.

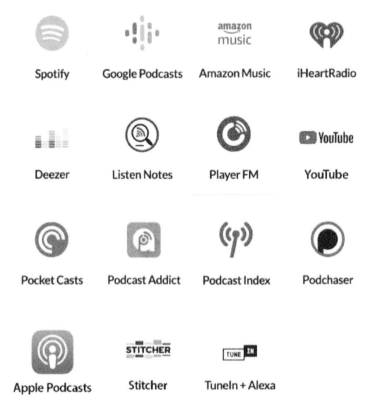

Spotify   Google Podcasts   Amazon Music   iHeartRadio

Deezer   Listen Notes   Player FM   YouTube

Pocket Casts   Podcast Addict   Podcast Index   Podchaser

Apple Podcasts   Stitcher   TuneIn + Alexa

Entrepreneurssource.com/podcasts

Launchpad:
LAUNCHPAD

Take Your Next Best Step
toward Your Career Revolution

The FREE online experience.

- **Find clarity about your professional future.**
- **Work at your own pace.**
- **Discover your path to a career you love.**

EntreprenurSource.com/launchpad

Social Media:

Connect on Social

Watch us on YouTube

Get the Business Insight on LinkedIn

See some pics on Instagram

Follow us on Facebook

Reviews and more at Google Business Profile

Tweet on Twitter

Listen on Spotify

Stay connected.
Get the tips, tools, and tactics you need.

EntrepreneursSource.com/social

ABOUT THE AUTHOR

Terry Powell is the visionary founder of The Entrepreneur's Source®, a world-class career-ownership coaching company. Committed to the development and advancement of those with a strong desire to become self-sufficient, Terry challenged the brokerage and franchise industry in 1984 and transformed conventional thinking about providing support and guidance to aspiring entrepreneurs and business owners and those who did not know what they wanted but knew that certainly there must be a better way to earn a living and live the life of your dreams.

Through his coaching practice and personal study, Terry discovered that 75 percent of adults have a strong desire to be self-sufficient. He also noticed that this desire did not equate to an interest in entrepreneurship, which many people fear. His focus on coaching and educating his clients about the possibilities available to them empowered them to find ways to pursue their Income, Lifestyle, Wealth, and Equity opportunities and experience independence in ways they could have only previously imagined.

Today, Terry continues to apply his knowledge and experience in the entrepreneurial community through mentoring, leading others to achieve their **Possibilities**, **Options**, and **Dreams**. His thought leadership has been widely featured in a variety of media outlets, including *The Wall Street Journal*, CNBC, ABC, and Bloomberg Tv.

In 1998, Terry realized that to make an even larger impact, he needed to empower other coaches to use the same powerful tactics and strategies he employed to empower his clients. Today The Entrepreneur's Source has Career Ownership Coaches across North America transforming the lives of thousands upon thousands of people who are seeking a better way to become self-sufficient.

ABOUT THE ENTREPRENEUR'S SOURCE

The Entrepreneur's Source® has helped over one million professionals explore their career possibilities with our powerful approach to education, awareness and discovery and our unique Income, Lifestyle, Wealth and Equity™ approach.

With over one hundred career ownership coaches across the globe, we strive to foster meaningful connections through earnest interaction, empowering aspiring entrepreneurs to identify, pursue and achieve their dream of self-sufficiency.

What makes us . . . *us*?

Community: We create a professional environment where coaches, clients and more come together to share, learn and grow.

Humanity: The people in our community are people, not numbers, quotas or statistics. We collaborate and inspire through empathetic, human interaction.

Integrity: We're steadfast in our mission to empower individuals as they prepare for the next phase of their professional lives.

Experience: For nearly 40 years, we have served our industry as a Career Ownership Coaching™ leader. We freely share the knowledge and wisdom we've gained to help people achieve their dreams of self-sufficiency.

BLOCKCHAIN
VERIFIED IP™

Powered by Easy IP™

Made in the USA
Monee, IL
08 July 2023